Defying Adversity as I Race to Achieve My Dreams

There Is Nothing Like Being Believed

Jennifer Wood

Hirschwood Press

MILL VALLEY, CALIFORNIA

© 2024 by Jennifer Wood. All rights reserved.

All rights reserved. No part of this publication may be reproduced, distributed, or transmitted in any form or by any means, including photocopying, recording, or other electronic or mechanical methods, without the prior written permission of the publisher, except in the case of brief quotations embodied in critical reviews and certain other noncommercial uses permitted by copyright law. For permission requests, write to the publisher at the address below.

Hirschwood Press
37 Bayview Terrace
Mill Valley CA 94941

Publisher's Note: Some names and other identifying details have been changed or omitted to protect confidentiality.

Defying Adversity as I Race to Achieve My Dreams: There Is Nothing Like Being Believed /Jennifer Wood. —1st edition.
ISBN 978-0-9973749-2-6 paperback
ISBN 978-0-9973749-3-3 ebook
Library of Congress Control Number: 2024904647

With Love

To my sisters and brothers,
CATHY, MITCH, KENT, AND LIZ
and
To their wonderful spouses,
DON, DEBORAH, AND DARRYL

And to
SUZANNE SALINGER
You brought dazzling experiences to my life.
REST IN PEACE, MY FRIEND.

CONTENTS

Introduction 1

1: November 22 & 23, 1963
The Promise to Myself at Age 12 15

2: Those Were *The Dazzling Days*
Three Life-Changing Events Washington, D.C. 1973 23

3: Where Did My Dazzling Days Go?
Horror Heartbreak Fear 41

4: My Exciting Life on Capitol Hill 65

5: The Doctors: *Van Ness, Neuro* & *Bland*
Is It a "Real" Disease? Or Is It About Paris?
or Do Ed and I Know Something? 79

6: The Dangers of a Misdiagnosis 105

7: 1994/1995 Dr. Cathleen E. Schmitt
She Believes Me 127

8: 2021: Secondary Progressive Multiple Sclerosis,
Moderate-to-Severe Range Oh No! 151

9: How Doctors Might Improve Their Diagnostic
Process and Communications With Their Patients 159

10: Dreams Come True Hyannis Port, Massachusetts,
1978 The Kennedys and The Salingers 169

11: The White House Staff 1979-1981 197

12: Back to California 1982 *and* Onward, Betty at Last .. 221

13: Letters & Photos of Dreams Coming True 231

14: Goodbye, Suzanne Salinger 241

15: How I Remember Madeleine Albright 247

16: Appreciating Clint Hill 257

Epilogue 263

Acknowledgments 279

INTRODUCTION

INTRODUCTION

It seems strange to write a memoir when you're not famous or prominent. I also haven't produced anything that's about to make a big splash and therefore justifies a glittering memoir.

Then why did I write this book? Why did my family and friends *encourage* me?

My mind is atwitter. Why?

Oh, yeah. The year 2021. It was a pretty bad year for me—in a **Damn!** *Here We Go Again* kind of way. Actually, the 2021 events were both way worse and way better than their predecessors. Interesting…. things got better *because* things got worse. **Crazy-making**. That theme sounds familiar to me, too. Crazy-making. Is that what my life has been about? Parts of it, for sure. But then so much of my life inspired my family and friends to excitedly await tales of my latest adventure, my latest accomplishment. I didn't disappoint! Hell, even *I* was excited by me!

This book is about my life. In so many ways, I've been so very lucky.

But then the bad came, and so unexpectedly. I was 22 when the *first* monster arrived.

Defying Adversity as I Race to Achieve My Dreams

I was fiercely ambitious and determined, part of a new wave of womanhood in the 1970s. Nothing could knock me off my exciting path, I thought. No, I *knew*. **Not going to happen.** I will not let anyone or anything stop me. *Moxie. Perseverance. Courage. Resilience.* These are my favorite traits. I employed them. Boy, did I have my work cut out. I expected sexism and misogyny in the workplace. My life's challenges involved so much more.

It might have been easier to cope and correct if the monsters had been *real* monsters.

But what if it's the nice professional waiting on you at a nice restaurant?

What if it's your psychotherapist who cares so much about you?

What if it's a doctor who's come to help? An illness that's mysteriously enveloping you? Acts of bravery and stoicism that are profoundly misunderstood?

What if it involves significant things you face about yourself that could possibly tarnish or even crush your huge and exciting successes?

On balance, my life has been wonderful. I think that's literally true, but I also try to emphasize the better

INTRODUCTION

parts (which doesn't mean I don't lose sleep or ruminate about the awful or lesser parts).

Maybe that's what this book is about: staying the course, not becoming vanquished when awful things happen. Taking charge. Knowing when to hold 'em and when to fold 'em. Feeling gratitude for your blessings. Emphasizing the positive.

I know I was blessed with lots of stuff from the get-go that other people don't have, but I bet lots of people with major challenges from the beginning would be surprised by what some of us comparatively luckier ones still had to face and conquer. Still try to face and still try to conquer.

So, off we go to take a look at my life. Can you learn something? I think so. Will you be smiling and laughing, too? Oh, yes. You will not be bored. (Wow. We need to talk if that happens!)

Thank you for taking the time.

INTRODUCTION

I've always remembered this. It happened nearly sixty years ago, when I was 13. My grandfather told me about a little boy's death. I was transfixed. My grandfather had read the story in a local newspaper. The wording on the boy's gravestone caught the community's attention. In addition to the usual—the deceased's name and dates of birth and death—this little boy's gravestone included, *I Told You I Was Sick*.

"I guess his parents didn't believe him. Or maybe they took him to the doctor and the doctor couldn't find anything wrong," I said to my grandfather.

"Yes, that's what I suppose as well," he replied.

I added, "And I guess they figured if the doctor couldn't find anything wrong, he couldn't really be sick."

"But then, the boy died. He obviously died of something," said my grandfather. "His family and doctor must have felt guilty they didn't believe him or help him."

Bless his heart, I remember thinking. *I Told You I Was Sick*. They gave him the last words.

I've thought a lot about that conversation with my grandfather over all these years. I sometimes wonder:

Did I worry I might have been that little boy if my circumstances had been just a little different?

I TOLD YOU I WAS SICK

INTRODUCTION

Some years later, in 1976, when I was 25, my mother and I had a memorable conversation. I was on vacation, back home from where I now lived in Washington, D.C., visiting my parents in Northern California. Mom and I were drinking tea at our dining room table. She'd just returned from visiting a long-time family friend in the hospital, a friend whose close ties to us were of the sort where my siblings and I called him "Uncle Walter."

He was only 67 and dying of pancreatic cancer. We were all so sad about his condition. He'd seemed so vital. Uncle Walter was very prominent in our community, in medicine as well as business. He had three medical degrees from an excellent college. Mom was emotional after her visit. What seemed to strike her most were the final words she heard from Uncle Walter that day. He looked so tired, Mom said, and then he sighed, "Oh, Ann, what I have learned, what I have learned." Mom's eyes moistened.

"Oh, that seems so sad," I said. "Did he explain what he meant?"

Mom said a nurse interrupted their conversation and Mom had to leave the room. Uncle Walter died quite soon after that day. We never learned what was specifically troubling him. We figured he was experiencing the vulnerability of being a patient in a hospital, being poked and prodded by busy medical personnel, facing frightening circumstances and procedures. Even though we figured Uncle Walter was getting the best care the hospital could provide—after all, this was the very hospital he'd been serving as a physician for years—it must have felt weird to have a role switch in that very place. Especially if you feel lousy and know you're seriously ill. He must have felt so out of control, as if the medical world was no longer his.

Whatever Uncle Walter meant, I knew I appreciated his thoughtfulness. I was reaching a stage in my own life where I worried that too many doctors—especially male doctors treating female patients—were highly deficient in something. Did they lack certain types of knowledge or empathy? Not listen to patients carefully? Have limited interest or aptitude in diagnosing seemingly "female" issues? Did they stereotype females as being weak, anxious, and quick to cry for help, so they didn't try as hard to help them as they might male patients?

I would have loved to talk to Uncle Walter about both of our medical crises. I think Uncle Walter's new insights might have been just what I needed to hear. I wish I could have comforted him, too.

THE SERIOUSLY ILL DOCTOR
SIGHED FROM HIS HOSPITAL BED:

OH, WHAT I HAVE LEARNED, WHAT I HAVE LEARNED

CHAPTER 1

NOVEMBER 22, 1963:
President Kennedy has been shot and killed
in Dallas, Texas

NOVEMBER 23, 1963
The Promise to Myself
at Age 12

CHAPTER 1: NOVEMBER 22, 1963

I bet most Americans who were born by about 1958 remember November 22, 1963. Whether Democrat or Republican or any other persuasion, that was the day when the 46-year-old president of the United States, John Fitzgerald Kennedy, was shot and killed — assassinated — in Dallas, Texas and the whole world seemed to react. There was television footage of his motorcade as it happily passed through town, the beautiful 34-year-old First Lady, Jacqueline Kennedy, smiling at his side. Their darling little daughter and son were waiting for them back at The White House in Washington. No U.S. president had been assassinated in decades since President McKinley was shot in 1901. It seemed unthinkable in 1963. The First Family was now heavily guarded by the Secret Service, the presidential car reinforced by the finest protection of the day.

President Kennedy's death on November 22, 1963, was probably shocking even for his detractors. For me, for my family, Oh My God. We were such enthusiastic supporters. My father and mother were devastated, heartbroken. For me, it was as if part of the world had come to an end. I almost couldn't stand it.

I can look back now, as I have done so many times in the sixty years since that day, November 22, 1963, and still feel the day slowly unfolding. It began as such a regular day. I kissed my parents goodbye before beginning my short walk down Golf Course Road to my seventh-grade class. Who could have guessed the next time I saw my parents we would all be in tears? Who could have guessed as my class broke for the lunchroom, our teacher, a man named Brooke Thomas, would bring us to immobilized attention once we returned?

Mr. Thomas, how I remember you. You got me so interested and experienced in debating as a 12-year-old; I ended up a Speech Communication major in college. You were such an inspiration to me. And of course, it was you, Mr. Thomas, who told me and my classmates about what happened to President Kennedy that day. I remember how you began. You calmly said you had something to tell us, something that was very serious, in a category close to the seriousness of a nuclear war. A drop of a pin could have been heard. Your tall body swayed as you spoke. Your shoe heels sometimes lightly tapped each other as you swayed. I knew you were trying to control your own emotions while handling this important responsibility of a teacher. I'm so grateful you were the teacher that day, Mr. Thomas. The day that changed so many lives all over the world in an instant was also the day your words changed mine. I have never been the same since November 22, 1963. It

CHAPTER 1: NOVEMBER 22, 1963

brought a line of demarcation to my life, the *before* and the *after*.

My feelings began to coalesce the next day, November 23, 1963. I was again walking to my seventh-grade class at Jacoby Creek Elementary School in Bayside, California. I remember that walk so clearly. Despite all the years that have passed, I can see myself walking down Golf Course Road, then cutting through a grassy, unpopulated area until I reached the houses in Bayside Heights. This was my usual path to school. This upcoming part is my clearest memory of that walk. I doubt there were many (likely not any) other girls at the age of 12 who had my thoughts—actually, my *worries*—as I walked down the final stretch: What am I going to do? *What am I going to do?*

Things have gotten so bad in Washington, D.C. in recent decades that it's almost impossible to imagine a U.S. president or U.S. senator inspiring people to better themselves—to study harder, join the Peace Corps or other volunteer organizations, get excited about all the possibilities that life holds if you try hard and keep on trying. But President Kennedy and later his brothers did just that for countless men and women throughout the United States and even throughout the world.

Defying Adversity as I Race to Achieve My Dreams

The Kennedys gave me the shivers. I turned cartwheels in my mind at the very thought of them. I didn't even know them, but they gave me confidence, joy, and inspiration. My aspirations grew through them. I didn't want a regular life. I wasn't exactly sure what I wanted to accomplish, but I knew it would be admirable and I would work among noteworthy people. Nothing could stop me. I couldn't wait to grow up and get started. I was so excited, so energized.

Now President Kennedy was gone. I knew as I walked down that little hill to my school I had to find a new anchor. I became fiercely determined at that very moment that I would get to know the Kennedys. I would find a way into the Kennedy orbit. I promised myself I would make that happen. I never told anyone about my plan out of fear I'd be laughed at. But, boy, did I tell myself. I *never* forgot that talk to myself that day.

It never occurred to me that health problems would play a significant role in my early adulthood, much less have any connection to my Kennedy dreams. I was healthy as could be at that time. But in just over ten years, in early 1974, at age 22, all hell broke loose. Just as I was actually realizing my dreams, I became frightened everything was falling apart. It helped that I'd read many books about John F. Kennedy and learned about his lifetime of health problems. His

CHAPTER 1: NOVEMBER 22, 1963

courage and perseverance guided me and inspired me to be brave and to not give up. As weird as this may sound, it is also very true.

I have a lot to tell you. Traumas began for me at the end of 1973, immediately after the wondrous first nine months of that year. Let's go back to the whole year of 1973. January through most of September comprise my most dazzling days. My dreams were coming true, sometimes without even trying. I was so happy. I doubt I will ever live such a year again. I want to tell you all about those dazzling days. Then I'll tell you about the traumas that lay ahead and how I handled them, how I'm still handling them.

The bad of my life has been, well, bad; kind of like hitting unexpected landmines. However, dazzling days always return. I think I'm determined to make them return, but I also think I'm lucky. My life is mostly composed of regular, overall good days. I am grateful and also lucky for those days, too. Let's go to my Dazzling Days of January to September of 1973. I'm smiling already. I think you'll smile, too.

CHAPTER 2

THOSE WERE
THE DAZZLING DAYS

THREE LIFE-CHANGING EVENTS

Washington, D.C.
1973

ULYSSES
Alfred, Lord Tennyson

…Come, my friends,
'Tis not too late to seek a newer world.
Push off, and sitting well in order smite
The sounding furrows; for my purpose holds
To sail beyond the sunset, and the baths
Of all the western stars, until I die.
It may be that the gulfs will wash us down:
It may be we shall touch the Happy Isles,
And see the great Achilles, whom we knew.
Tho' much is taken, much abides; and tho'
We are not now that strength which in old days
Moved earth and heaven, that which we are, we are;
One equal temper of heroic hearts,
Made weak by time and fate, but strong in will
To strive, to seek, to find, and not to yield.

THE ROAD NOT TAKEN
Robert Frost

Two roads diverged in a yellow wood,
And sorry I could not travel both
And be one traveler, long I stood
And looked down one as far as I could
To where it bent in the undergrowth;

Then took the other, as just as fair,
And having perhaps the better claim,
Because it was grassy and wanted wear;
Though as for that the passing there
Had worn them really about the same,

And both that morning equally lay
In leaves no step had trodden black.
Oh, I kept the first for another day!
Yet knowing how way leads on to way,
I doubted if I should ever come back.

I shall be telling this with a sigh
Somewhere ages and ages hence:
Two roads diverged in a wood, and I—
I took the one less traveled by,
And that has made all the difference.

CHAPTER 2: THOSE WERE *THE DAZZLING DAYS*

I had skipped a grade in grammar school, so I graduated from college in June of 1972, when I'd just turned 21. My cousin Debbie would be graduating from college a year later. We planned a trip to Europe shortly thereafter. To occupy myself in the interim, from January through July of 1973, I decided to move to Washington, D.C. to experience what seemed an interesting and exciting world. I didn't know anyone there but wasn't concerned. I planned to get a waitress job to pay the bills, but also to find volunteer work, perhaps on Capitol Hill. I'd heard living at a YWCA was a smart idea, so I sent a letter addressed simply to "YWCA, Washington, D.C." and was thrilled when I got a response. I was able to secure a room there for $50 a month, not including meals. I knew that was a deal even back then and eagerly took it. I'd been diligently saving money from other waitress jobs during college. It turned out this Y was located at 17th and K Streets, NW, an easy walk to the White House. My seven-month Washington experiment might be short, but I could feel my time in D.C. was going to be sweet.

How sweet it was.

Huge dreams came true for me in 1973 because of three unexpected events that happened as that year approached and as the early months of that year began. These events changed my life, with many reverberations felt to this day, **50** years later. Each of the three events alone would have gone a long way toward fulfilling my fervent wish expressed the day after President Kennedy's death, a wish to get to know members of the Kennedy family and to live and work among them and other important people. That all three events happened — and so quickly after college graduation and from such different sources — remains one of my life's happiest and luckiest mysteries.

The first event involves an older distinguished Frenchman, a professor and friend of my father's, Monsieur Gaspard Weiss, who was a founder of the Monterey Institute of Foreign Studies in Monterey, California (now known as the Middlebury Institute of International Studies). Monsieur Weiss decided (apparently of his own accord) that I should not go to Washington without a letter of introduction to someone of maturity and accomplishment who could look out for me, if necessary. He asked a friend for guidance.

This friend was none other than Jehanne Bietry Salinger-Carlson, the mother of President John F. Kennedy's popular Press Secretary, Pierre Salinger. Mrs. Salinger-Carlson apparently conferred with a number of people. Their consensus was that Barbara Gamarekian, one of Pierre Salinger's staff members in the White House Press Office and now with the

CHAPTER 2: THOSE WERE *THE DAZZLING DAYS*

Washington Bureau of the *New York Times,* would be perfect for the role. Barbara was my mother's age (45ish), divorced, without children, and very personable. She had previously been a legislative aide on Capitol Hill for Senator Hubert Humphrey and then handled press matters for President Kennedy. She was well-known for throwing parties at her lovely house in the historic Georgetown section of Washington, parties with good food and drinks and attended by other JFK staffers and highly placed Washington personages. And it was this Barbara Gamarekian who agreed to take on whatever role might be desired or needed during my seven months in Washington. She agreed to this role before I (and I think my parents) knew anything about Monsieur Weiss's activities. When I learned, I was stunned. I was touched. And I was thrilled. Yes!

Barbara Gamarekian was perfect for me. We immediately "clicked." Years later, her brother Glenn told me at one of her parties he thought Barbara saw a younger version of herself in me, that I was kind of a daughter figure to her. During my visits over the years, Barbara and I would sometimes walk up and down the streets of Georgetown. She'd point out all the houses currently or previously owned by the Kennedys and others of historic significance. We went to the movies together. I especially enjoyed being with her at the new Watergate movie so much in the news in 1976, *All the President's Men*. She invited me to several of her parties. I shook my head in wonder when a well-known JFK aide made a gin and tonic for me. I realized Barbara had been quoted many times in many of the books about John F. Kennedy that I'd been reading for years. I felt special knowing Barbara and seeing her interest in me. My confidence and aspirations grew in her presence. We stayed in touch all those seven months in 1973 and far beyond until cancer ended her extraordinary life at age 78 in early 2004. I tip my hat to Monsieur Gaspard Weiss and Jehanne Bietry Salinger-Carlson. Thank you!

The second of the three unexpected events happened in mid-December of 1972, a month before I was to leave home for Washington. I picked up the *Eureka Times Standard* (or whatever my local newspaper in Humboldt County, California was called at the time) and my eyes fell upon a story about an automobile accident in Delaware. An unspeakable tragedy had just struck the life of a newly elected U.S. senator from Delaware, 30-year-old Joseph R. Biden, Jr. He was to be sworn in as a senator just after I arrived in D.C. His wife and their three little children were out looking for a Christmas tree in Delaware when the accident occurred. His wife and one-year-old daughter were instantly killed. Their two young sons were now

CHAPTER 2: THOSE WERE *THE DAZZLING DAYS*

hospitalized and fighting for their lives. I took the newspaper to my mother. She read the story and looked stricken.

"Remember I said I wanted to find a volunteer job on Capitol Hill? This is it. I'm going to try to help this man." Mom asked how I expected to meet him or his managers. I said I had no idea, but I would find out.

Three months later, in March of 1973, a month before I turned 22, I became Senator Joe Biden's first Senate "intern." I had found his office in the Dirksen Senate Office Building on Capitol Hill and looked through the open door. A delightful middle-aged man greeted me. He turned out to be the Chief of Staff, Wes Barthelmes. I told him my background and desire to help as a volunteer. I'd gotten a Monday through Friday waitress job at a restaurant that only served lunch. Money worries eased when I found the restaurant also had a busy bar for the lunch crowd. Tips were very good. I told Wes I could work late afternoons and evenings during the week and anytime on weekends. Wes liked the idea of weekends. So that's how Chief of Staff Wes Barthelmes and I started working together on weekends. I answered mail, typed a speech for Senator Biden, helped organize the office—whatever tasks needed handling. The office was just getting up and running. Everyone was thunderstruck by the tragedy, including, of course, Wes.

Senator Biden was not in the office on weekends. He took Amtrak each night of the week to return to Delaware while his sons slowly recovered. He stayed with them all weekend. His sister Valerie stepped in to fill the maternal role until, years later, Senator Biden married Jill Jacobs (today known as Dr. Jill Biden, First Lady of the United States).

I worked weekends for nearly four months without ever seeing Senator Biden. His office was filled with pictures of him, his wife Neilia, and their precious little girl and boys. It was as if I worked in a mansion where I never saw the master. So, I felt special delight when Wes asked me one summer day if I would like to meet Senator Biden, to be placed on his schedule so the two of us could talk, before I left for Europe. Yes!

I was saving every penny for my two-month trip to Europe. I usually went to Capitol Hill by bus, but not this day. This day Senator Joseph R. Biden, Jr. was waiting for me in his office. This day, etched into every part of me, I put on my best outfit and hailed a cab. The sun was shining brightly as I watched the Capitol dome come closer and closer to the undulating car. I can still feel the tires. My eager eyes stared straight ahead. My face hurt from a bursting

CHAPTER 2: THOSE WERE *THE DAZZLING DAYS*

smile. Wes greeted me and ushered me into Senator Biden's office. I was 22 and Senator Biden, 30. (I'll soon be 73 and President of the United States Joe Biden is now 81. *Whoa. You're young and then*, ah, *not so much.*) I haven't the slighted idea what we talked about. But since neither of us has any trouble talking — no trouble at all — the conversation flowed easily for about 15 minutes.

When we were done, I walked down Capitol Hill to the Y. I had to work off my blazing excitement and energy. What a difference a few months can make. Rose petals fell from the sky.

The man who is now president of the United States sent me a handwritten thank you note at the Y before my departure. My adventure to Washington, D.C. was working out well. Very well, indeed.

I was so fortunate to have worked directly with any chief of staff, and with Wes Barthelmes, in particular. He was a mentor to me. He was a man of many experiences and talents. I had to smile when he told me he'd once served as Robert F. Kennedy's Press Secretary.

I'm so sad to say, Wes died of a brain tumor in 1976 at age 54. I'll never forget what he offered my life.

It's hard to believe that yet another, a third, spectacularly unexpected event would occur shortly after my arrival in Washington in 1973. It happened in February, a month after I arrived. It happened just after I first met Barbara Gamarekian and a month before I began my Biden internship. Get ready.

Picture a terrible waitress job, my worst *ever*. So bad, I quit after one week—and I don't quit easily. This was my first waitress job in D.C., just preceding the lunch-only one I would intermingle with the Biden internship. The restaurant was near Connecticut Avenue and close to the historic Mayflower Hotel. It was physically attractive and had good food and drinks, but my fellow waitresses later warned me it had been a "pickup joint" in a previous rendition. Foreigners now ran the replacement. It took no time to see and experience their brusque, sexist attitude in action. Then, on my first night, a patron came up to me and eagerly said, "I'll give you $40."

"Excuse me?" I responded, with all the (genuine) innocence in the world. He dashed out the door. What? Another waitress, who'd watched the interaction, explained. Apparently, word hadn't adequately spread that we were no longer *that kind* of restaurant. I pondered the situation. I silently laughed, too. Even in 1973, I thought *only* $40 was rather insulting. Whoa. I just Googled it. $40 in 1973 would be $245 today — a tiny bit better. But *no!* I was a virgin and certainly no pickup chick (*or prostitute)*!

I decided to quit that job at the end of the week.

Then the most amazing thing happened.

The *very first* person I waited on the first night at that restaurant brought a slice of *Kennedy Heaven* to my life. It is still — a half-century later — almost unbelievable. I would learn the handsome, distinguished-looking 48-year-old man I waited on was Joe Velletri. He lived on Capitol Hill. Joe was the warm and friendly type who asks seemingly sincere questions of many people. He asked me about me. I said I was from Arcata, in Northern California, and had just graduated from college there. I added that I was happily killing time in D.C. while waiting for my cousin to graduate from college; that we planned a late summer trip to Europe. I probably added that I'd arrived in Washington in mid-January in time to see the Nixon Inauguration. I bet I also said I wasn't a Nixon fan, but figured why not see a presidential inauguration if you can. I know I didn't say a word about the Kennedys or Salingers. So you can imagine my shock when Joe turned to his friend and said, "You know, Ed, we ought to introduce Jenny to Suzanne." "Who's Suzanne?" I asked. "Do you recall

President Kennedy's Press Secretary, Pierre Salinger? Suzanne is his daughter. She's your age."

Holy Moly. When I told Joe and Ed that I'd actually come into town with a letter of introduction from Pierre Salinger's *mother* to a woman who'd worked for Pierre at the White House, they were stunned. Then I was stunned (and thrilled) when, within one day, I received a call at the YWCA: "Hi. This is Suzanne Salinger."

"Wow, that was quick!" I responded. With deliciously droll humor, Suzanne responded, "Well, I just *have to meet* the cocktail waitress who came into town with a letter of recommendation from *my grandmother*. I just have to meet you."

I laughed.

Let me tell you more about Suzanne's grandmother, the mother of President John F. Kennedy's very popular and widely known Press Secretary, Pierre Salinger. Her very name suggests a lot: Jehanne Bietry Salinger-Carlson. Bietry was her maiden name. "Salinger" was added when she married Pierre's father, a New York engineer named Herbert Salinger, and "Carlson" was added after Herbert's early death and her remarriage to Jerome Carlson. Jehanne Bietry Salinger was a French journalist who spent most of

CHAPTER 2: THOSE WERE *THE DAZZLING DAYS*

her adult life in California—in San Francisco and later in the Monterey-Pacific Grove area near Carmel. She was the author of several books and newspaper articles and frequently gave lectures on art exhibitions. She served as editor of *The Argus*, a journal of art criticism, which was published monthly. You can Google her name and find sophisticated, rather exotic photos of her. In other words, Suzanne Salinger's grandmother was, well, unlikely to spend her days barhopping with Cocktail Waitress Wanda or writing letters of recommendation for her.

I laughed at Suzanne's words and also clarified that I'd gotten a letter of *introduction*, not recommendation, from her grandmother and that we didn't even know each other; a mutual friend had arranged it. I added I'd just finished college and had many career aspirations. I said I'd enjoy meeting her—and hoped my clarifications hadn't reduced her interest.

"I want to meet you," Suzanne declared. Yes!

Well, Hello Suzanne Salinger. A few days later, she drove from her apartment in Virginia and picked me up at the Y. Off we went to Capitol Hill and the famous Monocle Restaurant, known for happily serving food and drinks and drinks and drinks to members of the U.S. Senate and House, their spouses and girlfriends, and their staffs; U.S. Supreme Court Justices and—well, you name it. (Years later, when I worked in the Russell Senate Office Building for Senator Edmund Muskie—a stone's throw from the Monocle—my eyes fell upon a unique celebrity there. It was none other than the beautiful actress Elizabeth Taylor with her new husband, Senator John Warner.)

Suzanne and I hit it off right away. We talked and laughed easily. I found her warm and devilishly fun. I think we both got a kick out of how we met. We went to the Monocle many times over the months, as well as to her other favorites, such as The Dubliner—also on Capitol Hill—on St. Patrick's Day and Mr. Smith's in Georgetown. I loved them, too.

Wonder of wonders, Pierre Salinger was expected in Washington the next month, in March, from his current home in Paris. He'd apparently enjoyed the story of his mother and me and told Suzanne he'd like to take us to dinner at Sans Souci, the new Washington "in" spot across from The White House. What a night that was. Henry Kissinger was also dining there and came over to our table to greet us!

Imagine the reactions of my parents and siblings as they tried to absorb the wondrous experiences that seemed to be falling into my lap. They (and my other

CHAPTER 2: THOSE WERE *THE DAZZLING DAYS*

relatives and friends) got such a vicarious thrill. I don't think I ever stopped smiling.

To this day, a half-century later, I bet many of my family members and friends think Suzanne Salinger and I met through the likes of Barbara Gamarekian. That would have made sense: Barbara worked for Pierre Salinger for years. But Suzanne and I met because of that awful waitress job that I quit after a week, because the first person I waited on asked me a few innocuous questions and decided his friend Suzanne and I might enjoy knowing each other. The rest is history, as they say. And I have lots more to tell you — for example, about a trip Suzanne and I made to Hyannis Port, Massachusetts in 1978, spending the night at the Kennedy Compound and going sailing on Nantucket Sound with Ethel Kennedy and many of her (and Robert Kennedy's) children. But I'm saving the best for last!

Now it's time to turn from the dazzling Washington, D.C. days of January to July of 1973 to my cousin Debbie's and my trip to Europe. It was our first time there and lasted about six weeks. The trip was the stuff of our dreams. Indeed, it was so wonderful, I jumped at the offer of my friend Lynn to return with her shortly after Debbie and I got back to the U.S.

Lynn's traveling companion had to cancel at the last minute, so off she and I now went to Paris!

Lynn's and my travels in Europe also made wondrous dreams come true.

That is, until the nightmare evening arrived.

CHAPTER 3

WHERE DID MY DAZZLING DAYS GO?

HORROR
HEARTBREAK
FEAR

A RAT CAUGHT
IN A MAZE

CHAPTER 3: WHERE DID MY DAZZLING DAYS GO?

How could 1973, that wondrous year, end so cruelly? How could 1974, 1975, and 1976 add more cruelty and weirdness? The magic of January to September 1973 crashed into the grotesque by year's end. I was determined to rise beyond it, not to let it vanquish me. My adulthood was just getting started!

My father perfectly captured what my life felt like to me as late 1973 merged into the next year and the next and the next: a rat caught in a maze.

My cousin Debbie's and my dream trip to Europe in late 1973 was wonderful. It was our maiden voyage to Europe, and we ended up exploring ten countries. We were on a tight budget and mostly stayed in youth hostels. The hostels were a mixed bag. The crummier ones (dirty, poorly maintained) wouldn't pass muster if we were older, but they weren't so bad for energetic, excited 22-year-olds. We were enthralled by the beauty and historic wonders in each country. We loved the ease of the Eurail Pass as we moved from country to country, and we enjoyed seeing American actress Lauren Bacall in a London stage production of *Applause*. It was adventure after adventure.

Paris was an anticipated highlight. My father, who died in 2008, was Dr. Frank B. Wood, foreign language professor extraordinaire at Humboldt State

University (now known as California Polytechnic State University, Humboldt) in Arcata, California. He knew five languages—French, Spanish, German, and Italian, as well as English. He created the Foreign Language Department at Humboldt and taught those first four languages during his 33-year tenure there. His Ph.D. was in French. France resided in his heart. He visited Paris several times, either alone or with Mom. Their sabbatical to Paris was a lifetime highlight. My sisters, Cathy and Liz, speak French fluently and delight in Paris, that City of Light. Debbie and I found it heavenly, too.

I was thrilled to return to France soon after Debbie and I returned to the U.S. Ha! How could I say no to my friend Lynn when her traveling companion had to suddenly bow out of their vacation plans? So, off Lynn and I went in late September.

We thoroughly enjoyed several days in France, and Paris in particular. But then that city, of all cities, brought horror and heartbreak to our lives. "We'll always have Paris" make wondrous words in the movie *Casablanca*. Lynn and I will always have Paris, too, but for both heavenly and horrifying reasons. I know I shouldn't blame a city or allow the actions of two French men to color my perceptions of that city or country. But that is easy to say. I've heard the Kennedy family long avoided Dallas, Texas, after

President Kennedy's assassination there. People need to protect their psyches and hearts when they know *that is the place* where the dreadful deed occurred; that is the place inhabited by those two men, men who cast a shadow over the rest of our lives.

On our final night in Paris, Lynn and I decided to have an early dinner at a little outdoor place near our hotel. The food wasn't very good, so we didn't finish it. We decided to try another restaurant located even closer to the hotel. We ordered wine.

Our waiter seemed to be taking his time. When a friendly American couple sitting next to us had to rush off to an event, they offered us the rest of their small carafe. We happily took it. It didn't take long for the other wine and our dinners to arrive. Two waiters were serving us. My parents had made it very clear we shouldn't be flirtatious in any way or overly friendly with men in France. My elegant mother recalled the look of utter disdain she received in Paris from a middle-aged male professor when she simply offered a small polite smile as she looked his way. Apparently, he took that as a most inappropriate "come on." (Dear God.) Suffice it to say, we did not flirt, have much eye contact, or act too friendly with the waiters.

All Lynn and I know is not too long into our sipping of the wine and eating, the world inexplicably changed for both of us, pretty much simultaneously. It was as if strobe lights were going off—flashing white lights everywhere. We couldn't imagine what was happening. We weren't by any stretch drunk, plus we knew enough about being drunk on alcohol to know this wasn't part of that process. We were also too naïve then to even think we'd been drugged. We just knew we wanted to settle the bill and get out of there, get to our nearby hotel. We did that.

Things then became awful. I remember Lynn being very sick and vomiting. There was no bathroom in our hotel room, so she had to run back and forth from our room to the hallway restroom. I wasn't physically sick but was otherwise feeling very strange; I kept passing out. I kept thinking I had to help Lynn but would fall back on my bed and pass out again. We don't know if it was five minutes or five hours later, but our hotel room door opened, and the two waiters entered. The door must have been unlocked because of Lynn racing back and forth to the hall restroom.

The waiters left Lynn alone. Whatever they put in our drinks made Lynn so violently ill, she was "going at both ends" all night and she was physically (and emotionally) impaired for days.

CHAPTER 3: WHERE DID MY DAZZLING DAYS GO?

I became their target. Their drugs seemed to make me into a rag doll. I would hear something and could only try to react. I remember Lynn vomiting on the hotel room carpet and wanting to help her, saying her name, and trying to reach out, but then falling back on my bed, passing out again. The men proceeded. I was a 22-year-old virgin. I will always remember their laughter as they caused me excruciating pain as they ripped me open. They spoke in French while they laughed. I think they were laughing about how hard it was to penetrate me. Their game was on now: they proceeded through my anguished cries, through my repeated No's, until they both succeeded.

The rapists then left us with two more memories.

Lynn and I woke at the same time in the early hours of the morning. Panic set in. In the first few seconds, I remembered: *Something terrible has happened. We've got to get out of here. Hurry! Go, Go, Go.* As I frantically put on my (white) bra, I noticed something blue. What? Blue ink. The rapists had signed their first names on each strap, preceded by "Love," as in: *Love, Jean-Paul.* I thought Lynn would vomit again. "How sick are those guys? Imagine doing this, too," I spat out, vile feelings enveloping me.

Then, once we returned to the U.S., Lynn had her pictures developed. (This was a different era, when cameras required film and then film to be developed.) As Lynn looked through her pictures, she paused at one and was grateful she was alone. One of the waiters had clearly used her camera. The picture was of me. I was passed out on the twin bed. I was naked, with a sheet seemingly staged to (sort of) cover my breasts. The bra was draped across me.

When Lynn told me about her discovery and showed me the picture, I could barely conceive how awful some people could be.

Not anymore. I have spent the rest of my life trying to cope with how certain groups of human beings are treated. I was drawn to the political world more than anything else by my rage at the way people of color were treated in the United States and elsewhere, as well as by the horrors Jews have known (among others). I hoped to work among leaders whose aim was to find and implement legal and social corrections.

From an early age, I was alert to discrimination against females, but I increasingly realized the devastating dimensions of this mistreatment. Females comprise half the population of the entire world. They bring human life into the world. Despite this, they are so often denigrated and cruelly treated by

CHAPTER 3: WHERE DID MY DAZZLING DAYS GO?

the world — even by blood relatives and those who are supposed to love them most dearly.

I want to cry out to all the perpetrators: *Why? Who are you? Are you so weak you have to hurt people to feel better, so insecure you think cruelty will solve your problems? Don't you know your actions show the world who **YOU are**? I bet you're sometimes a reasonable, even good person. I also bet in the depths of your being, you know your actions are all too often like those of a ferocious animal. Don't you think Karma is waiting for you?* Don't you think Karma *should* be waiting for you?

BREATHTAKING WONDERS
HEARTBREAKING SHADOWS ~

I'LL ALWAYS HAVE PARIS

CHAPTER 3: WHERE DID MY DAZZLING DAYS GO?

Lynn and I were grateful we'd prepaid our hotel bill. That allowed us to race outside after throwing our clothes on and grabbing our backpacks. We caught the first train to Luxembourg, as previously planned, and splurged on a nice hotel room in an effort to comfort ourselves. After several vulnerable days, I think Lynn and I were able to enjoy the rest of our time. It certainly helped when I got my period and knew a pregnancy wouldn't add another nightmare. I learned that this "get into a different gear and press on" ability seemed to come to me naturally. It would also serve me well in the coming years as I tried to carry on with my career dreams while also coping with a growing array of physical problems that defied accurate diagnosis or respectful medical discussions and validation.

When we returned to the U.S. around mid-October, Lynn immediately flew to her home, while I spent some time with relatives in the Boston area. I spoke enthusiastically about Europe. That was easy to do because so much of what Debbie, Lynn, and I experienced overall was fantastic. I had no desire to discuss the horror in Paris. It was clearly on my mind; I thought about it a lot. But I didn't want to cast a pall on my excursions. Young women were just starting to assert themselves in this way: traveling without a man, feeling free to explore the world. If someone were to say, or imply, we shouldn't have been allowed by our parents (or the world) to do this, I think I would have completely lost it. Females were sick and tired of being controlled, their activities and rights restricted, because of the proclivities of some males. That's punishing the victim.

I next enjoyed visiting my grandparents and other relatives in Maine. After a week or so, my grandparents drove me up to Montreal. I took an interesting train ride across Canada to visit my sister Cathy and brother-in-law Don and their two little girls, Rebecca and Vanessa, in Alberta, where they now lived. I *did* tell Cathy and Don about Paris. They were very concerned and caring, and I appreciated their comforting words.

Then came my final travel of the year, to Arcata, in Humboldt County, California, for Thanksgiving and Christmas with my parents, brothers Mitch and Kent, and sister Lizzie. Our family home was actually in Bayside, an unincorporated town a few miles from Arcata that typically provided additional land with each house purchase. Our lovely home sat on over an acre, which Dad filled with gorgeous trees and other plants, including a magnificent rose garden. Mom filled the house with beautiful bouquets throughout the year. We also had a house and yard filled with cats and sometimes a dog, rabbits, chickens, a donkey and, briefly, a lamb—among other interesting

CHAPTER 3: WHERE DID MY DAZZLING DAYS GO?

creatures. Our holiday celebrations were wonderful. Mom was a great cook and always decorated the house beautifully. I had no desire at all to mention what happened in Paris. I knew the time *might* come, but felt I was handling it as well as could be expected. Plus, I wanted all of us to enjoy Thanksgiving and Christmas and for the otherwise glorious year to end on nothing but a happy note.

It's still hard to believe all that happened in 1973.

I'd decided, as my Washington, D.C. days waned months earlier, that Washington was the ultimate place for me. It almost felt as if the city loved me even more than I loved it. And I really loved it! But I thought I'd try out another city just in case.

Since I'd had success with the YWCA in D.C., I researched the same in San Francisco. I learned that the YWCA on Powell Street, right across from the famous Fairmont Hotel on Nob Hill, was a good place for both men and women. So I secured a room there (I think for only $65 a month — including meals) and that became my new home in January of 1974. I lived there through August.

The Y was a definite winner. I met many interesting people there — travelers, such as myself, as well as the likes of men who worked for the San Francisco engineering company, Bechtel. My understanding was these men actually lived in other parts of the country most of the time but had to be at headquarters periodically. The Y became their second home. We had a fabulous chef. He loved surprising us with an amazing array of foods. I'll never forget the surprise luau. The delicious pig was a big hit.

The Y was beautifully located. The Fairmont Hotel was across the street with, among other attractions, the Tonga Room. The Mark Hopkins Hotel was a stone's throw away, with its Top of the Mark for cocktails, and then there was a nearby corner bar where everybody soon came to know everybody (kind of like the TV show, *Cheers*). I knew from many youthful travels to San Francisco with my family that this was a beautiful and fun city, but I also quickly knew Washington, D.C. was the place for me. I missed the *substance* of the life there (at least true back then). Washington felt like the center of the universe, where the president and other national leaders, the Supreme Court, top news people and organizations resided. I wanted that life. But San Francisco felt right for the next several months, and I was pleased to find a temp job at a land title insurance company on Bush Street. It was an easy walk from the Y.

Then a day arrived in February that became the beginning of the end of life as I'd always known it.

CHAPTER 3: WHERE DID MY DAZZLING DAYS GO?

This was early 1974, when I was still 22. My 23rd birthday wouldn't arrive till the end of April. I was sitting at my desk performing my interesting yet simple tasks at the title insurance company. Suddenly, the skin on my back felt as if it was on fire. It felt exactly like a bad sunburn over most of my back. I'm fair-skinned (lots of Irish in me) and I flush easily. When I went into the restroom to check things out, I expected to see a very red, blotchy back. But my back looked normal—no red, no rash, nothing at all unusual. I couldn't fathom it. I returned to my desk. The burning feelings continued. I waited a long while before checking again until I felt confident that *this time* the look would correspond to the feelings. But again, nothing abnormal. I thought I should feel relieved that nothing showed, but I knew something weird was happening. That thinking continued over the next several days, when the skin burning seemingly flipped from my back to the front of me, to my mid-section. Once again, *nothing* appeared. It didn't feel like an internal problem, just the skin. About two weeks later, the burning stopped. But now prickling, tingling, and crawling sensations developed on my arms, shoulders, back, my front mid-section, and even eventually on my face. They came and went unpredictably. The crawling sensations were by far the worst. It felt *exactly* like bugs were crawling on me. These skin **feelings** (not visions) lasted on and off for years. I frankly don't know how I survived them.

Over the next several years, I saw several physicians for this supposedly strange malady, starting in March 1974 in San Francisco. When I moved back to D.C. in October of that year, my quest for help continued, also to no avail. My experience with the first doctor in San Francisco will give you the flavor of these encounters.

About a month after the burning, prickling, and crawling skin sensations began, I asked people at the Y if they knew any good doctors in San Francisco. Someone recommended an internist practicing near Van Ness Avenue whose office was walkable from the Y. I'll call him Dr. Van Ness. He seemed pleasant and caring at first. I told him my symptoms. He ordered a full blood panel and urine tests, and, eventually, an upper and lower Gastrointestinal (GI) Series. (Magnetic Resonance Imaging—MRI—technology was either non-existent or in its infancy at the time.) I easily passed all the tests. Dr. Van Ness became very upbeat. Nothing serious is wrong! It's probably just a stress reaction that will subside once I understand my symptoms are stress-induced and not serious. I told him I wasn't under stress. He repeated I'd passed all the tests, so there was no medical basis for my symptoms. I just needed to reassure myself and I should start to feel better soon. I thanked him and left his office.

CHAPTER 3: WHERE DID MY DAZZLING DAYS GO?

I thought about Paris. That was, of course, extremely stressful and awful. Maybe the repercussions of being raped were now attacking me in this way. That made me even angrier at the cruel power the rapists exerted over me. But no matter how much I tried to think this might be the answer to my physical problems, my instinct shouted: That's *not* it. You've got a medical disease. It's going to get worse, too.

I felt cast adrift. It seemed other doctors were going to say the same thing. This issue was talked about among women—how doctors often threw a stress diagnosis at them—way before doing the same to males. Medical studies showed this was true. My problems were also embarrassing. While the future would bring many non-skin symptoms, the dominant one in the initial months was a sensation of bugs crawling on me. Try telling that to folks—family, friends, *and* doctors.

I floundered for weeks over what to do next.

Then one night at the Y, the crawling feelings woke me. The sensations had never been this bad. They were all over my back, shoulders, and arms. I looked at myself in the mirror, splashed water on my face, and felt terror. Absolute terror. **What is happening? What could this possibly be?** My heart raced. I walked over to the window facing San Francisco's famous Pyramid Building. I stared and stared at that grand building. I almost felt I was talking to it. I had to catch my breath. **DAMMIT! Tell me why this is happening! THIS IS GOING TO BREAK ME! I can handle pain, lots of discomfort. But I can't stand these bug feelings. They're going to ruin everything. HELP! SOMEONE!** *Please, please* **help me.** I cried the hardest I'd ever cried in my life.

After a while, I sat on my bed and took deep breaths. I was shaking. Then I ordered myself to think. **Think.** I knew I had to figure out a rescue plan, or I was on my way to an emotional crisis. An idea suddenly came to me. I calmed down and even felt energized. Here's what I realized: Dr. Van Ness doesn't even know me! I'm only 22 years old and he probably thinks I'm some young, hysterical, whining, anxious type who rushes to the doctor at the drop of a hat. Hell, that's the *opposite* of me. But *he* doesn't know that! I'll make another appointment with him and explain. Then he'll take me more seriously and either figure out more tests to order or refer me to a specialist. Yes! I'll call him on Monday. I felt so much better.

I made the call on Monday and saw Dr. Van Ness later that week. I practiced what I would say to him. I practiced the words and my tone of voice, until I felt confident he'd have a different—a correct—perception of me. And he seemed to listen to me very carefully. I

CHAPTER 3: WHERE DID MY DAZZLING DAYS GO?

told him I was a stoical person, that when I said my symptoms felt "terrible" I was, if anything, downplaying their severity. When I was done, he flashed a smile at me and said in a singsong voice, "Oh, that's just *terrible, terrible, terrible!!!*"

Dear God. Did he think I was a three-year-old crying over a boo-boo on my knee?

I quickly walked out the door. That was the end of Dr. Van Ness for me.

I saw one other internist in San Francisco. His blood tests also yielded nothing. He said he didn't know what was wrong. As with Dr. Van Ness, he didn't suggest or make a referral to any type of specialist.

I decided to take matters into my own hands. Lacking the Internet services that assist us today, I felt lucky to find a good bookstore around the corner from the title insurance company. I'd wolf down my lunch at the office and spend the rest of the hour reading medical books. *Crawling Sensations of the Skin* led my hunt. I was greatly relieved to find you don't need to be a nutcase or drug addict to experience them. Occasional blurry eyesight was just beginning to occur. So, I threw that in the mix. (There were a few other symptoms as well.) Bit by bit, my research kept coming up with the neurological autoimmune disease

Multiple Sclerosis (MS). I didn't (yet) have balance or falling problems, but the more I read about MS, the more I believed that was what I had. I also learned that each case of MS is different.

I told my parents about my findings. They were frantic and wanted me to come home and see our family doctor or a specialist in Arcata. I said I'd decided to stick with my plans and return to D.C. There were lots more physicians in Washington—top specialists—and a return to my magical place might be just what I needed.

There was no effective treatment for MS (at that time), so I wanted to get cracking on my career. Yes, my symptoms could be awful, but I compartmentalized well, shifted into another gear and pushed on while at work. I could let emotions flow once I got home. I felt I was fighting against time. MS could be crippling, among other destructive things, and I didn't have time to waste. I appreciated Mom and Dad's huge worries, but wild horses couldn't have stopped me from continuing with my plan.

And Washington, D.C. in 1974 greeted me with the same exciting embrace as Washington, D.C. in 1973 had done. Additional big dreams were quickly realized once my plane landed at Dulles Airport in October.

CHAPTER 4

MY EXCITING LIFE ON CAPITOL HILL

CHAPTER 4: MY EXCITING LIFE ON CAPITOL HILL

Senator Biden's Chief of Staff, Wes Barthelmes, was very welcoming when I returned in 1974. There were no openings on Senator Biden's staff, but Wes arranged for me to prepare a resume at his office and offered to serve as a reference. I pounded the pavement between the Senate office buildings and those for the House of Representatives, dropping off my resume in some instances and getting interviewed in others. I was thrilled when I received an offer from Maine's acclaimed senior senator, Edmund S. Muskie. I would serve as his receptionist for the first six months or so, starting in late October 1974, and then as a Research Assistant and Legislative Correspondent (writing Senator Muskie's answers to constituent and national mail) for the next four years. I was only 23 and my career was happily clicking along!

I found a wonderful apartment on Capitol Hill. It was at the top of a small townhouse located very close to the Capitol Building, the Library of Congress, and the U.S. Supreme Court Building. The large studio contained a back deck, and the front window offered a clear view of the Capitol Building. Friends were concerned about my high rent. Fasten your seatbelts: the rent was $235 a month! Others were paying around $150, but I knew I could afford it with my new annual salary of $10,268 as a full-time staff member for Senator Muskie. And I loved the apartment. I could easily walk to work. I figured I'd be living there for a long time. D.C had rent control, too. Indeed, when I decided to return to California in 1982, my rent at that same apartment was the *envy* of my friends: $335 a month.

An added future delight was that some co-workers on Senator Muskie's staff would eventually become prominent national and international figures. Who could have guessed Madeleine Albright—her desk very close to mine—would one day become America's first female Secretary of State? Or Chris Matthews would host an admired TV program called *Hardball* for many years? Or two other co-workers, my close friends, Fran Miller and Dolores Stover, would become the personal secretary of Senator Ted Kennedy in back-to-back succession? Senator Kennedy, nearly fifteen years younger than his brother, John F. Kennedy, had an office on the fourth floor of the Russell Senate Office Building, while Senator Muskie's office was on the first. I often saw him in our building (where both of his brothers had also had their offices). Fran and Dolores and I stayed special friends until the end of their lives many years later. They both adored Ted Kennedy. I, of course, loved knowing they felt that way.

It felt so good to be back in D.C. But there was one big issue. My physical problems remained and gradually grew worse. Even though I increasingly believed I had MS, there was still a tiny part of me that had hoped my simply being in magical Washington would cure me. My disappointment was huge.

My strength in dealing with my health issues was diminishing. I remember an awful day in early 1975. I was busy as Senator Muskie's receptionist, handling the phones and office visitors. For no discernable reason, my skin sensations and strange vision issues were extra bad. I found it extremely difficult to compartmentalize—to switch into work mode. I couldn't wait for the workday to end. When that time arrived, I practically raced to my nearby apartment. I don't know if the problems were actually worse than normal or if I was simply at the end of my rope trying to handle things. I entered my apartment and covered my face in blankets to muffle my cries for relief, for someone to truly help me. I then raced into the bathroom to once again employ the only skin relief method I had discovered: immerse my body fully in water, any temperature, and the crawlies would almost instantly disappear. When I was in a lighter mood, I'd joke to family and friends that I was thinking about becoming a fish. That night, I fell asleep in the bathtub. I'd stayed in the tub for hours, long enough for the skin sensations to settle down, even when I got out of the tub. This "temporary water cure"—whether in warm or cold water—is apparently a medical mystery. I've asked doctors. No ideas. Whatever, I'm grateful to have inadvertently discovered it, at least for me. I hope for others, too.

I now had great health insurance working at the U.S. Senate and decided it was more than time to search for a neurologist. One came highly recommended. I first saw him in the spring of 1975. I had just turned 24. I'll call this neurologist Dr. Neuro. Just like Dr. Van Ness, he initially seemed empathetic and interested in me. He performed all kinds of manual tests and agreed MS was a possibility. That both relieved and frightened me. I hungered to get an accurate diagnosis and to find at least some relief from my symptoms. To be taken seriously by a neurologist was almost thrilling—it was validating and certainly welcome after the condescending display by Dr. Van Ness. But nobody wants to have MS.

Dr. Neuro ordered a brain scan and a spinal tap. Unfortunately, Magnetic Resonance Imaging (MRI) technology wouldn't become an MS diagnostic tool for many years.

Experiencing the spinal tap itself was a piece of cake for me compared to its aftermath. Dr. Neuro performed the tap in his office, not in a hospital. I told him I'd take a cab home. He only cautioned me to lie

CHAPTER 4: MY EXCITING LIFE ON CAPITOL HILL

down as much as possible or else I might get "a bad headache." He had previously given me a prescription for a painkiller just in case. I was only slightly worried. I felt I was in good hands.

I decided not to tell my friends or co-workers about the tests until sometime after I got my results. I felt I'd opened up too many health discussions in San Francisco. It became overwhelming. I took one day off from work "to handle some personal business" and took a cab by myself to the appointments.

I like doing lots of things by myself, but that decision on spinal tap day was not my wisest. It was a very hot and humid June day in D.C. For some reason, the cab I ordered from a phone booth (no cell phones then) outside Dr. Neuro's office failed to come when expected. I foolishly waited and waited, standing in that sweltering weather, before calling the cab company again. By the time that cab arrived, I'd stood or sat for at least an hour in the heat before I got home to lie down. I thought I'd lucked out when I didn't get a headache right away. I called my parents and was sincerely upbeat. However, the headache later hit like a thunderbolt. It felt like knives were stabbing me from the top of my head downward. The painkiller was definitely not strong enough.

I discovered the headache would completely stop if I was lying completely flat. But I had to periodically get up to use the bathroom or eat. I called Dr. Neuro's office and told the staff what was happening and why. The doctor took many hours to call me back. He then said things should get better soon. But after three days of this, with no relief, I called Dr. Neuro again and insisted on being hospitalized. He agreed. My mother said she'd fly out from California, but I assured her hospitalization would quickly fix me, plus other nearby relatives and friends were now aware and kindly reaching out. I was taken by cab to George Washington University Hospital, lying down on the back seat.

I was so glad to be in a hospital. I needed help big-time, and the hospital gave me a vastly better painkiller. Then my eyes fell on a line in my admitting paperwork. It said, "Diagnosis: Multiple Sclerosis."

OMG. Careful what you "wish" for. I started trembling. Of course, I didn't *want* to have MS. I just believed I had it. I wanted a *correct* diagnosis and treatment. I then wondered why Dr. Neuro hadn't delivered this news to me in person. Between that question and rumblings I was overhearing from hospital personnel that spinal taps should only be done in a hospital, I started to think I had pathetic doctor karma.

CHAPTER 4: MY EXCITING LIFE ON CAPITOL HILL

Dr. Neuro arrived in my hospital room many hours later. He was cheerful and said he'd heard I was upset about the admitting diagnosis. He clarified he had to provide a diagnosis for me to be admitted to the hospital, but that he hadn't actually reached that conclusion yet. He said George Washington was a teaching hospital, so he would have a group of other neurologists work on my case, too. That sounded like an excellent plan to me. I thanked him and got a good night's sleep.

Several doctors besides Dr. Neuro talked to me and manually examined me over the next couple of days. I heard my proteins were somewhat elevated in the spinal tap. Then Dr. Neuro offered their final conclusion: I did **not** have MS or any other medical problem. My problems were "functional." He asked if I understood what that term, functional, meant. I said I did (at least at that time, a mental health issue). He asked if I had any questions. I said I didn't and thanked them all. I took a cab home.

I was emotionally spent. At least the headache was gone. And I was proud I'd advocated for my hospitalization.

It turned out Dr. Neuro had one more surprise for me. I was in a very excited mood several weeks later, still serving as Senator Ed Muskie's receptionist. His schedule included an office visit at 10AM from newspaper correspondent and columnist, Charles Bartlett. Anyone seriously interested in President Kennedy knew about Charlie Bartlett and his wife Martha. They were the couple who introduced Jack Kennedy to Jacqueline Bouvier at a dinner party at their Washington home in 1951. The four became close friends. I couldn't wait for ten o'clock to arrive. My job was to greet Charles Bartlett and then announce his arrival to the senator's personal secretary, Dolores Stover. But my joy that morning turned to tears when the phone rang at 9AM. My health insurer informed me my entire multiple-day hospital bill in response to the spinal tap fiasco and the neurology assessment wasn't going to be covered.

"Why?!" I cried out. "It was supposed to be covered at 100%."

"We need your doctor to confirm the services were medically necessary. We can't get him to call us back. We've repeatedly told his staff about the urgency in receiving his approval. Tomorrow is the deadline." I frantically called Dr. Neuro's office and begged them to get him to respond ASAP. I readily discerned their own frustrations with Dr. Neuro. Fortunately, the insurance rep was sympathetic to me.

CHAPTER 4: MY EXCITING LIFE ON CAPITOL HILL

"It sounds like it was medically necessary to me. What is wrong with some doctors?" Dr. Neuro at last called him back at the end of the last day. I don't know if Dr. Neuro was grossly insensitive or actually sadistic. I'm told there is some kind of plaque or similar honor for Dr. Neuro in a Washington, D.C. medical building. Maybe he provided better treatment to patients he thought had "real" diseases.

I decided to give a medical diagnosis one more shot that year. No physician directed me towards them, but I decided to see an endocrinologist and a rheumatologist. After testing, both also ruled out conditions in their specialties. One of these men was extra noteworthy for this: After he joined the "I can't find anything wrong" group, I sighed and said, "Okay. I guess I should see a shrink."

The room became silent for a few moments. Then he calmly said, "I kind of wish you hadn't said that." *What?* "The people who need mental health treatment are usually the ones who refuse it." I explained some might have perceived me as such a patient, but I genuinely disagreed this was about a mental health issue. I didn't want to waste time and money going down the wrong diagnosis and treatment lane. I reminded him I worked at the U.S. Senate. Undergoing **psychological** treatment could (at that time) raise job-threatening red flags. He nodded as if he suddenly had new insights.

I believe this was the same doctor who had a curious look on his face at another point when I said I was planning a vacation. I stifled a defensive response in case I'd misread him. Was he actually wondering how I could go on a vacation if my symptoms were so bad? Or was I becoming paranoid around male physicians? I decided to add, "Fun and relaxing vacations are so important for everyone. I'm sure you doctors agree for yourselves as well! My physical problems have been unpredictably appearing and disappearing for so long now, I don't expect a vacation to help in that regard. But vacations certainly can't hurt and are a good distraction." He seemed to agree. There was his wordless nod again.

I spent Christmas of 1975 in California with my family. Mom and I conferred with our long-time (and admired) family doctor. He also ruled out a medical issue but told me **not** to seek mental health counseling. He cautioned, "If you think there are incompetent doctors out there, you can't imagine how bad some mental health professionals can be." He felt I could figure out my problems and get better by taking a serious look at myself. (OMG. I kid you not. I would have accomplished that long before if it were so straightforward.)

But, of course, I increasingly also had to wonder, more thoroughly and deeply than ever, was I being ridiculous? Was I *in denial?* Denial *in neon lights?*

At last, I decided to seek psychological counseling. I knew whatever my health problems were (*and I still gravitated to MS*), I was so confused that emotional support and guidance from a professional felt relieving. I also figured I'd get brownie points from future physicians if I could say I'd officially explored mental health issues. **Whatever.**

I just wanted relief.

Mine was an increasingly lonely journey. I tried to appreciate how hard it must have been for my family, friends, and co-workers to hear all these medical details without their also having plenty of questions and opinions. I started to receive (mostly unsolicited) suggestions about how I should find the right guy, fall in love, get married, and have babies. Some said maybe I needed more religious or spiritual guidance, or maybe I was taking the wrong approach to living my life (whatever that meant). People meant well, I think, but the suggestions became demoralizing and demeaning. I thought I was living a magnificent life, an admirable life, my dream life, until this damnable health thing happened. And I thought I was amazingly brave.

Now, as my father surmised, I felt like a rat caught in a maze. A good rat caught in a crazy-making maze.

I decided to choose a *psychiatrist* (versus another type of mental health specialist) because that meant he would have a medical degree, plus specialization in psychology. (Few women held such positions then.) A co-worker arranged for me to meet with her psychiatrist friend. The psychiatrist heard my medical history and said, yes, I could be helped through his specialty. I liked him, but wasn't sure if I was relieved, skeptical, or insulted by his assessment. Perhaps all three! Unfortunately, he was fully booked, but he gave me a list of Washington psychiatrists he recommended. The last person on the list also turned out to be the only one available. (I hoped that wasn't an omen.)

CHAPTER 5

THE DOCTORS:
"DR. VAN NESS"
"DR. NEURO"
&
"DR. BLAND"

IS IT A "REAL" DISEASE?
OR
IS IT ABOUT PARIS? OR
DO ED AND I KNOW SOMETHING?

MY FUTURE FEMALE PSYCHOTHERAPIST
SHOOK HER HEAD AND SAID:

"DR. BLAND MUST HAVE GONE TO
SIGMUND FREUD HEAVEN WHEN
YOU WALKED THROUGH
THE DOOR."

CHAPTER 5: THE DOCTORS

I saw "Dr. Bland" (not his real name) twice a week for three years, starting in the spring of 1976, when I was 25. He was a middle-aged Freudian psychiatrist. As the weeks went by, he advised me to stop talking about MS. He said the medical community had judged against my having it or any other medical disease, so I needed to focus elsewhere. (Indeed, my first insurance claim carried his diagnosis: Anxiety Neurosis with a Psycho-Physiological Reaction of the Neuro-Musculo-Skeletal System.) Dr. Bland seldom said anything—not a thing—even when I spoke of complicated or emotional matters. (I guess Freudians, at least back then, wanted you to figure it out mostly all by yourself. That may sound wise to some, but I totally disagree. At least sometimes, Speak, Guide, Offer insights! Then let patients assess and react.) Since I didn't know what could be causing my health problems from a mental health standpoint, I started talking about my life from the beginning. There were lots of wonderful, happy, and very loving experiences there. In so many ways, I'd had an idyllic childhood. There was nothing Big, Bad, and Traumatic—not until the rape in 1973. So, I told him about Paris several weeks after I started therapy.

Dr. Bland listened very intently in his big, comfortable chair, smoking a pipe, while I spoke with obvious, yet controlled, emotion. I told him I had been a 22-year-old virgin. I told him about my parents' admonition not to flirt, have much eye contact, or be overly friendly with French men, which my friend Lynn and I carefully followed. I told him about the restaurants, the food and wine, and the two waiters, and about how a sudden "strobe light" began flashing for both Lynn and me. I discussed Lynn's violent vomiting and diarrhea attacks that resulted from whatever was put in our wine and how she raced back and forth to the hallway restroom at our hotel. I said I kept passing out, coming to, and passing out again—I felt like a rag doll. I discussed the confusing laughter as the two men spoke French while they both tried and tried to penetrate me, about the excruciating pain of the rape, how I cried out from the pain and issued multiple No's. Then I told Dr. Bland about their writing their first names in ink on my bra straps, preceded by the word "love." I finished by telling him about the semi-pornographic picture Lynn had discovered they'd taken of me with her camera, a picture of me passed out, partially naked, with that bra draped over me.

I was noticeably shaking when I finished. My teeth were chattering. I felt exhausted and blew my nose. Given his history, I was surprised when Dr. Bland spoke.

Very calmly, he looked at me and said exactly one thing: "Did you enjoy it?"

CHAPTER 5: THE DOCTORS

I almost go berserk every time I think about that moment.

Years later, I (separately) asked two female psychotherapists if they could imagine asking a female rape victim such a question. They both said, **NO.**

I have no memory at all of what I said to Dr. Bland. It is possible I only glared at him.

I do know he never communicated anything even remotely like that to me again.

MY PSYCHIATRIST ASKED ME
ONE QUESTION ABOUT BEING RAPED:

DID YOU ENJOY IT?

CHAPTER 5: THE DOCTORS

Dr. Bland did handle one situation very effectively. At some point, perhaps a year later, when I was 26, I talked to him about men I had dated or was dating and my sex life with some of them. Perhaps he discerned my lack of passion or romantic feelings. He simply asked me one day, "What about women?" My stumbling response said a lot to him and to me.

I had reached a point of such desperation about my health issues, I would have considered having an exorcism. I was willing to consider anything, face anything, no pride, no shame, no fear. Well, only sort of no fear.

Denial is an amazing thing. Back then, an ambitious man or woman certainly did not want to be gay. It may be hard for some people in today's world to imagine or remember, but gay people could be denied entry into some colleges and businesses simply because they were gay. They could have been celibate, but they were still gay. They could be fired or denied promotions because of it. A decorated soldier with multiple years of honorable military service could be *dis*honorably discharged from the military and lose his pension and other benefits if the military simply found out he was gay. He (or she) didn't have to be caught in any sex act. This was very scary and especially wounding to those of us who were earnest and hardworking, as well as trying to accomplish admirable goals. Many of us tried desperately not to be found out.

Many learned to run from themselves. That was made easier if one could easily pass as straight. I moved and dressed like a feminine straight woman. That was genuinely me. I also wasn't attracted to masculine-appearing women. The only women I knew or assumed were gay appeared masculine to me. They might be wonderful people, but they were not attractive to me in a romantic or passionate way. That made it easier for me to run and hide from my sexuality as I focused on my other burning desires and ambitions. I poured myself into work and accomplishments and having fun times with my straight friends. I only dated men. I felt most comfortable when I was among straight (or seemingly straight) people.

I'll tell you an illuminating story. After 4½ years of working for Senator Muskie on Capitol Hill, I decided to pitch for a job on the White House Staff. Vice President Walter F. Mondale (President Jimmy Carter's vice president) had an opening in his Advance Office in the sprawling Old Executive Office Building located across the driveway from the White House. I was hired as his Advance Coordinator. (More on that later.)

CHAPTER 5: THE DOCTORS

One of my favorite Advance Team Members was a tall, handsome man I'll call "Ed." Women drooled over and adored him. He and I became friends. My job was to coordinate logistics for the vice president's domestic and foreign travels. I sent Advance Man Ed out on many trips to prepare for the vice president's arrival. I'd not seen Ed for many months when he returned to Washington at one point. He called to say he was coming over to my office and I should be prepared. He said he'd gained 100 pounds and was embarrassingly overweight. I tried to make a joke about eating junk food on the road, but he stopped me. He said he gained the weight on purpose.

I knew we needed to talk. Maybe I knew what he was going to tell me. Maybe I thought Ed and I were alike. Indeed. He also easily passed for straight. He had no shortage of female interest in him, as I had no shortage of male. He wanted children, as I wanted children, which was then largely only open to heterosexual unions. He was professionally ambitious, and I was the same. He came from a large, loving family, just as I did. We didn't want to upset or disappoint our parents, grandparents, or our siblings. We worried about what our aunts, uncles, cousins, and friends might feel or say. We had been warned that our (straight) friends might dump us. Maybe our families, too. Ed and I were largely used to delighting people. We loved that. Potentially having the opposite effect—

breaking a parent's heart, disgusting, or angering people significant to us—especially over something fundamental to who we actually *were*, was devastating. And all the while we were also displaying such magnificent career success. Ed and I hobnobbed among U.S. presidents and vice presidents, as well as other top national and international leaders. Movie stars, singers. Pope John Paul II at the White House! We were inside the White House all the time. I became a White House Staff Member at the age of 27! Famous leaders loved having Ed as their Advance Man.

Talk about Cognitive Dissonance: Am I a Success or Am I a Failure? Are you thrilled by my accomplished life or are you filled with shame, disappointment, and fear now that you know I'm gay? Is everything tarnished now?

How did Ed and I feel about ourselves? We internalized the world's homophobia, just as other gay people and their families, friends, and co-workers so often did (even if unconsciously). After all, we all lived in the same world.

I think Ed and I constantly fought an avalanche of emotions, perhaps even more than we realized. Some came from within, from the internalizing of homophobia. Then the world just kept throwing daggers. Ed had once served as an advance man for a highly respected U.S. senator who was actually more famous for his career prior to entering politics. He told Ed more than once that his affection and respect for him were such that he considered him one of his sons. Of course, that compliment warmed my friend's heart.

Then came the 1984 Democratic National Convention in San Francisco. Vicious anti-gay slurs spewed from this U.S. senator's mouth as he and Ed and other prominent people drove through San Francisco. Ed had no idea the man held such extreme views. Once again, Ed stuffed his feelings and proceeded with his job. As people of color (who can pass for white) know all too well, even if you can fake it outwardly, you will still feel the prejudicial dagger striking you. And faking it is itself punishing. It wears on you.

Ed gained 100 pounds in an effort to make his tall, handsome physique unattractive to the males he found so sexually and romantically appealing. He punished himself.

I didn't want anyone, including myself, to truly find out about me. But Dr. Bland's question and my desperation to find the source of my health problems made me decide to finally open my eyes. Good Lord, maybe I'm gay and *this* is the "MS" culprit! Face the truth, deal with my homophobic issues and, poof, my health problems will stop.

I started laughing out loud in my apartment one night. Am I romantically and sexually attracted to (some) women? Duh. I even intentionally went out of my way to walk by certain females way back in my school days because they turned me on. I *knew* they turned me on. I knew I did this, but I didn't put the gay label on it. That was too risky for my huge career ambitions and too psychologically threatening for me. Who wants to be in the "loser" group, the *pervert* group? I didn't know any gay women (that I was aware of) and the ones I assumed might be gay weren't my type; they appeared mannish. At that point, I know Ed had been dating women and not particularly enjoying sex with them. The attraction was just not there. In a similar way, men were simply not attractive to me sexually or romantically. The best I could do was date men I found handsome and nice and who appeared to be going places professionally. Those factors kind of worked for having "an exciting date" for a while. But once I actually fell in love with a couple of women, as I did in my late twenties, faking it with men really didn't cut it. The contrast in emotional and physical feelings was profound. Plus, I broke a couple of men's hearts when I said goodbye (gently, I hope) without disclosing the real reason why. Pretending can be confusing and unfair for everyone.

CHAPTER 5: THE DOCTORS

Then, around 1978, at age 27, just as I was finally facing my sexuality with Dr. Bland and worrying about telling my parents and siblings, a "Gay Bomb" dropped on my family. And it wasn't even mine. Totally unexpectedly, my brother, Kent, who is 6 ½ years my junior, disclosed he was gay. He was in tears with our parents because his boyfriend (whom we thought was simply his friend) had broken up with him. He was heartbroken and needed family support but couldn't receive it without disclosing the full truth. This surprising news almost made me scream. I felt compassion for Kent, huge compassion. But at the same time, I had (then) never heard of more than one gay person coming from the same nuclear family. I started to freak out for all of us. We were an Ozzie & Harriet family—normal, happy, educated, delightful. Many people told us they wished they were part of our family. *Dear God, what is happening?* Then, since I was increasingly thinking my health problems stemmed from my negative feelings about being gay, I began worrying my symptoms would worsen. I also felt extra protective of Mom and Dad about their potential sense of failure or disappointment, especially if they knew two of their five children were gay. I gave love and support to Kent, but I (briefly) reverted to more actively dating men, more actively faking it—again.

I didn't have to imagine what my parents might feel or say about me if I told them I was gay; I heard their reactions to Kent's disclosure. They were always loving but displayed confusion and fear. My parents were progressive Democrats, very focused on civil rights. But, especially back then, having a gay child could be confusing and difficult even for the best parents. My family went through a tough time. I waited almost seven years—until 1984, when I was 33—to disclose my sexuality to my parents. I waited until some healing had occurred over Kent and the deaths of Mom's parents and her sister Sally. (I had told my siblings earlier.) Such a disclosure is seldom easy, and it never seems to be the right time for it. But such honesty is critically important, especially in a family as open, trusting, and verbal as mine. It's *not* about your *sex* life. It's about your *romantic* life, your "*settling down*" life.

"You're such a pretty girl, Jenny. Anyone special in your life?"

"Can't find Mr. Right? Don't be too picky!"

"Better catch the bouquet at your friend's wedding! Your biological clock is ticking away, too."

How many times did I hear such comments from a variety of people? Then I made the mistake of

CHAPTER 5: THE DOCTORS

purposely exaggerating my feelings for a guy I'd recently met at a resort in Maine. I did it to help settle those comments down. It had the opposite effect. An excited interest took off like a rocket. When he turned out to be a handsome psycho, I heard admonitions about poor judgment; the romance lasted *two weeks* and I was the one to end it! I soon learned to stop talking about the men (even good ones) I was making myself date. I think my mother, a great romantic, assumed I hadn't found my guy because I was afraid to let myself go, to be vulnerable to romantic love.

If so, oh no, Mom. Finding the right *woman*, as well as facing and then disclosing this huge gay secret, was my vulnerability. And, for me, in that era, it was an especially huge vulnerability.

I had been very much in love with two women by this point, but only Kent knew about them. That's another deep vulnerability in-the-closet gay people have to contend with. Your jump-for-joy romantic happiness, your luscious relationship contentment — and your romantic irritations and heartbreaks — are undisclosed to many important people in your life for years. Sometimes for a lifetime.

My disclosure in 1984 at age 33 was initially difficult for my parents. I think my wonderful mother might have taken the news personally because of the old psychiatric stereotype that *the mother is at fault* for her child's problems. If she did feel that way, it breaks my heart. No one is at fault. There is no fault. And Mom really always knew that, too. It takes time for people to handle controversial and complicated issues. Gay people certainly know that. By the time most of us (at least in previous eras) felt ready to disclose to family and friends, considerable time and often excruciating effort had been expended to handle our own adjustment to the truth.

Then we had to steel ourselves for what our disclosures might bring.

As if that weren't enough, an emerging nightmare was in the news about gay people, as well as others, in the early 1980s. It hit my family within the first couple of years of my moving back to San Francisco from Washington, D.C. in late 1982. My brother Kent told me he had strange swollen lymph nodes in his neck. He and his doctor worried he might have the mysterious new disease increasingly presented by gay men. I only vaguely knew what he might be talking about. Kent said gay men were suddenly losing huge amounts of weight, wasting away, and dying. Even young, previously very healthy, gay men. It was just too awful to digest. Kent, as always, looked handsome and healthy as could be. He resembled blue-eyed actor Paul Newman and was

CHAPTER 5: THE DOCTORS

enjoying his life and popularity in nearby Sonoma County. Very tan and fit. No way he could be seriously sick. *No way!*

Way. It was just the beginning of the dreadful disease that had no name. Then "HIV" and "AIDS" would all too soon be known throughout the world. Kent has bravely and diligently battled the disease since that time. We're thrilled he recently celebrated his 66th birthday. His good fortune seems to stem at least in part from the steady development of AIDS drugs that worked for him, as well as his strong constitution.

We never forget the precious souls who weren't so fortunate. Some endured rejection by their families just when they needed them most. There was a growing societal cry that AIDS was God's punishment for being gay. (Never mind that other groups of people were also battling this initially mysterious disease and that sex between women was soon recognized as "safe" or at least "safer" sex.)

There's more. I had always dreamed of having children. I loved them and wanted to be a mother. I looked forward to experiencing pregnancy, that creative miracle, too. If anyone had told me I would never be a mother, I would have screamed.

Several obstacles developed. Where could a gay woman find a father for her baby, especially in that era? What complications might that bring—for the child and the father and me? A sperm bank? Can I handle and afford all this? Then I thought, why not find a gay male friend, someone who would make a wonderful father? Two such friends were *very* interested. But the growing HIV/AIDS crisis sent chills through us. Accurate testing for the disease was in its infancy. As Kent's health worsened and the destruction caused by AIDS became increasingly real, I grew increasingly cautious. I worried about the infection status of prospective gay fathers and about the safety of sperm banks.

My worries were heartbreakingly validated when both the interested men died quite swiftly from AIDS. Dear Gary and Ed have been gone for decades now. Some medications that helped Kent hadn't been developed when they were alive, while others didn't work for them (or caused awful side effects). What a loss in every way. It was also a lesson for me. Careful. *Careful.* I then developed an uncontrollable bleeding fibroid tumor that required a full hysterectomy. This, of course, ended my ability to become pregnant. I explored adopting in the early 1990s, but then other health issues arrived in 1994-1995, along with older age. I took the hint: I cherished my nieces and nephews and great-nieces and great-nephews even more.

CHAPTER 5: THE DOCTORS

My older sister Cathy and her husband Don began the parade of grandchildren Mom and Dad so embraced, the children who made aunts and uncles out of my siblings and me, with the arrival of their four: Rebecca, Vanessa, Sarah, and Christopher. The youngest of us all, Liz, and her husband Darryl were next with their sons, Jeremy and Ryan. Then the oldest of my two brothers, Mitch, and his wife Deborah offered us a thrilling surprise. When they were both 52 and had been married for twenty years, they realized they should have adopted years before, after pregnancy efforts had been unsuccessful. So they announced one Thanksgiving at my house they were at last going to start the adoption process. Their dream was to adopt two somewhat older children who, ideally, were siblings. It didn't take long for sisters Maddison ("Maddie") and Lucille ("Lucie") to become their daughters. Even the judge at their adoption ceremony showed emotion that wonderful day.

As the years have gone by, the children of the children have entered our family picture. They now happily include McKenna, Chace, Gabriella, Julien, Leo, Wyatt, Lyla, and Beau.

And when my partner, Betty Hirschfeld, came into my life in 1987, our lives became blessed by Sacha and Elianna, the son and daughter of her brother Richard and his wife, Leigh.

We love being aunts and great-aunts.

It's so good that the world has gotten better in many ways about gay issues.

I'm happy—and not at all surprised—to say my parents and others in my family got way past the initial concerns about Kent's and my sexuality. When Kent told the rest of our family about his HIV/AIDS health crisis, everyone totally embraced him. Indeed, our parents lovingly reached out to several of Kent's friends with HIV/AIDS, especially when they learned about the limited or lack of support from their own families. This included some friends they had not previously met.

And when Betty became part of my life, the seas parted. My parents, siblings, and other family members and friends easily adored her. Betty's parents readily connected with me and the rest of my family. The same was true for Betty's brother and cousins, and their spouses and families. It has all worked out.

I had to stifle a smile periodically over the years when my parents expressed anger or incomprehension over

CHAPTER 5: THE DOCTORS

homophobic beliefs or actions. They didn't seem to remember their own initial questions and notions.

I think the idea that gay people "choose" or "decide" to be gay runs deeply in ingrained (and often unconscious) homophobia. Why do that? Why *be* like that? You'll have a terrible life! *If we keep pounding that into you, you won't be homosexual anymore!*

Such ideas would almost be funny if they weren't still so prevalent and dangerous all over the world.

I'm delighted to say Betty and I have been in a loving, happy, and committed (finally legal!) partnership for over 37 years.

Kent, as well as Cathy and Don, Mitch and Deborah, and Liz and Darryl and their families are also thriving. We are very close and miss our parents so much. Dad died at nearly age 86 in 2008 and Mom at 92 in 2020. We're so grateful to always feel them by our side.

CHAPTER 6

THE DANGERS OF A MISDIAGNOSIS

THE EXPERTS SAY:

NOTHING IS MEDICALLY WRONG.

Nothing
is
Medically
Wrong.

OFFICIAL DIAGNOSES FROM MY DOCTORS

They have all been discredited.

"Stress"	Internist "Dr. Van Ness" - San Francisco	Not a medical issue
"I Don't Know"	Internist #2 - San Francisco	But he offered no referrals
"Functional"	Neurologist "Dr. Neuro" and several other neurologists	Not a medical issue
	George Washington University Hospital – Washington, D.C.	Not MS
"I Don't Know"	Endocrinologist & Rheumatologist – Washington, D.C.	But they offered no referrals
"Jenny does **not** have MS or any other medical disease. She should think long and hard about how she's living her life."	My family's otherwise admired doctor – Arcata, CA	"No, she shouldn't see a mental health professional. If you think there are incompetent doctors out there, you can't imagine how bad some mental health professionals can be."
"Anxiety Neurosis with a psycho-physiological reaction of the neuro-musculo-skeletal system"	Psychiatrist "Dr. Bland" - Washington, D.C.	
"Central Serous Retinopathy — Caused by Stress"	Ophthalmologist "Dr. Blind" – San Francisco	

CHAPTER 6: THE DANGERS OF A MISDIAGNOSIS

Have you ever thought about the consequences of a misdiagnosis? For example, on the physical side, a patient might needlessly die or undergo unnecessary surgery or *not* receive important surgery. A patient might have to cope with pain, discomfort, and disability — a worsening of health — all of which might have been avoided by a correct diagnosis and proper treatment.

Then there is all the wasted time, effort, and money, as well as the emotional toll on patients, their families, friends, and their medical team when misjudgments about what is happening prevail. This leads to errors not only in treatment plans, but in assessments about the very personality and character of the patient. Let's see how.

One day I (politely) asked my doctor (after I'd passed all his recommended tests and he'd concluded there was nothing "medically" wrong), "Is it possible medical science needs to develop different tests for my condition or that we need new testing devices?" He offered a wan, silent smile.

His ears might have perked up and he might have even apologized had he lived another twenty years. That was when, **in 1994, twenty years after the onset** of my symptoms, I at last received an accurate, demonstrable diagnosis. MRI — Magnetic Resonance

Imaging—scans, among other technological advances, led the way. (My goodness—new Testing Devices! I offer that above-referenced doctor my own special smile.)

Let's look at some possible diagnostic "challenges." This will involve one of my favorite subjects, *Crawling (and Other) Sensations of the Skin*. Let's pretend we have:

Patient #1, *proven* by blood tests, etc. to have *Type 2 diabetes*;

Patient #2, *proven* by MRI, spinal tap, etc. results to have *Multiple Sclerosis (MS)*;

Patient #3, whose condition is *judged* by her doctors to be psychosomatic ("not medical") because she has passed all the *known* or *applied* "medical" tests, and yet she **says** she still feels her symptoms.

Diabetic Patient #1 feels comforted by the frequent TV and magazine ads she sees for ***diabetic neuropathy***. She doesn't feel so alone when she's reminded about the common ***nerve damage*** that can result from diabetes. Patient #1 says: "I can't stand ***paresthesias***—*burning, tingling, prickling, and crawling skin sensations.*" She's excited to try the neuropathy treatment being advertised. Relief is coming!

CHAPTER 6: THE DANGERS OF A MISDIAGNOSIS

MS Patient #2 overhears her. "*Paresthesias* can drive you nuts. I think my doctors thought I was a nut before the **development of MRI Brain and Spine Scans**. Doctors can finally **see** all the **lesions** in my brain and spinal cord. MS tests show my *burning, tingling, prickling, and crawling skin sensations* come from *nerve damage.* MS caused parts of the **myelin sheath**, the fatty covering surrounding my nerves, to **burn off**. Everyone now understands that I'm brave!"

Patient #3 exclaims, "*What*? My doctors say my skin symptoms are **hallucinations!** They say my *burning, tingling, prickling, and crawling skin sensations* are called '*formications*' and I need **psychoanalysis.** Why are mine 'hallucinations' but yours are 'real'? People seem to think I'm a whiner or hypochondriac who '*needs help.*' Really? I used to think I was stoical and brave, too. I feel dismissed and minimized."

There are, of course, those who suffer from hallucinations or physical problems resulting from the likes of stress or profound emotional and mental disturbances. Psychotherapy and psychoanalysis can be very helpful for them. Most people could probably benefit from a good therapist. Most of us have emotional "baggage" from just living our lives. Therapy can provide clarifications and coping mechanisms.

There has been a growing understanding in recent decades that we shouldn't separate medicine into *medical* (physical/biological) versus *mental* (psychological/behavioral) health issues. Since they all reside in a single body, in a single person, "biological" and "mental" issues are actually interactive. We've learned in my lifetime much more about body chemistry and how the chemistry of one's brain affects one's perceptions and actions. Psychiatrists have increasingly used a growing array of medicines—*psychotropic medication*—to help with psychological issues. Sometimes these medications even replace Talk Therapy.

The fields of neuroscience and psychology can actually complement each other.

Think about this:

Maybe hypothetical Patient #3 really does suffer from hallucinations and psychological treatment is a wise emphasis. Unlike the **actual nerve damage** and the associated actual nerve reactions experienced by Diabetic Patient #1 and MS Patient #2, maybe Patient #3 incorrectly surmises she also suffers from their skin symptoms. Maybe Patient #3 is unconsciously converting her emotional and psychological troubles into seemingly less threatening physical symptoms for which there is no demonstrable physical cause.

CHAPTER 6: THE DANGERS OF A MISDIAGNOSIS

Maybe when she's ready to face and deal with her deeper issues, her skin troubles will subside. **Maybe.**

In declaring this, part of me wants to sarcastically say, *Right: Such Woo-Woo Therapy.* But of course, these things can happen. I know a woman who went through a long period of actually choking because of her strong feeling that she had a throat obstruction. Her doctors could not find anything physically wrong. Psychotherapy helped her enormously. All her symptoms subsided. And that is wonderful.

But think about this:

How would you like to actually be someone like Patient #1 or #2 (suffering from diabetes or MS) — but the whole world surmises you are (that weirdo) Patient #3? What might that do to your psyche? To your sense of self? To your strength and ability to cope with your very real and serious physical illness? How do you handle potentially learning there were medications to treat your illness, as well as to provide physical relief, medications that could have slowed or stopped your disease progression — if only you had received the correct diagnosis?

At least two (male) doctors referred to me as the patient with the "vague" symptoms. I tried to be articulate and precise: the burning skin on my back felt *exactly like a bad sunburn; the crawling felt like numerous actual bugs were crawling on my skin.* Burning and tingling/crawling sensations develop from many disease processes. "Vague?" Are you kidding me?

Dismissive doctors teach patients not to believe in themselves, not to trust their instincts or their **knowledge**. Patients bit-by-bit absorb: "You are wrong. Listen to us. We know, you don't. Don't waste our time." This can be crazy-making for a patient.

Alfred Hitchcock might say, "Ah! This is such glorious gaslighting! Imagine being gaslit by your very own doctor — the very person who swore he would *Do No Harm* to his patients! Let's make a movie!" Now, I'm not saying I experienced interactions of this caliber. But I (and other women and men) have experienced interactions close enough to this "Hitchcock movie" that I know the medical profession needs significant repairs. *Both* male and female doctors can be criticized (and praised). I have friends who vastly prefer seeing male doctors. I appreciate this, even as my experience at least with this illness starting in 1974 directed me otherwise.

Also, I was recently hospitalized for several days. All the doctors were male. All but one nurse was female. The nurses seemed to be in their 20s to 40s. I told them I was thinking about writing this book — a book

CHAPTER 6: THE DANGERS OF A MISDIAGNOSIS

discussing how numerous male doctors in the 1970s, 1980s, and 1990s told me nothing was wrong with me medically. I asked the female nurses if a significant number of male doctors could still be characterized this way—as arrogant "know-it-all" types, who were often patronizing and dismissive—*especially to females.* I added that I was not only including their interactions with female patients, but female nurses and female doctors.

OMG! Yes! Yes! Yes! Five female nurses (every single one I asked) said, "You need to write that book." One even sought me out after I left the ICU for a private room to repeat: *"A book like that is so needed. Please write it."*

How pathetic is this, especially after decades of "conscious-raising" about how badly women are so often treated in the workplace by males. **And this was a *hospital.***

What is it with some men? Are they truly arrogant— do they *truly* believe they're superior to females? (Not that "superior" people have the right to be rude or mean.)

I think many men profoundly fear the perceived strengths of *other males* (they fear they *can't compete* with them) and they fear females because of their *dependency* on females to meet their sexual and/or emotional needs and desires. Many try to control and limit the lives and education of females, as well as minimize female strengths and accomplishments, in order to compensate for their own insecurities. They commit acts of violence to put and keep females "in their place," thereby supposedly effecting a superior place for males.

The patriarchy set this all up so well, especially for white, heterosexual males. Males wrote the rules and then stamped them as authoritative: males are superior and in charge, females are at best secondary and the lesser gender. *Really?*

I've asked female surgeons how male doctors treat them. Often with disregard or disdain, I've been told, especially by *older* doctors. (Are they afraid of something?)

I wonder why more females don't live with greater confidence—even strut their stuff. I'm not even talking about the knowledge and skills, for example, of female surgeons. Think about this fact: **Females create human beings within their very own bodies**. Then females deliver those full-fledged human beings (eyes that see, ears that hear, hearts and brains that function magnificently) to the world. Males contribute a profoundly important ingredient—

CHAPTER 6: THE DANGERS OF A MISDIAGNOSIS

sperm—to the creation of a human being. But the female body supplies the corresponding profoundly important egg—and *then everything else* involved in the nine-month human creation process—including breasts that supply nourishment to the infant. **Can anyone argue against this as the most creative and powerful accomplishment in human life?**

Are some males threatened by this? Are some females so diminished by the world, they don't fully recognize their own breathtaking strengths and achievements?

The world indeed minimizes and even obscures the **maternal baby-making prowess** (among numerous other accomplishments), while exaggerating the male role—saying the pregnant woman *carries* the baby for nine months, after the *male has gotten her pregnant*. Ah, more accurately, the pregnant woman spends months in an **elaborate physical process** provided only by a female body, a process that allows a full-fledged human being to be created, progressively developed, and then born from the union of the female's egg and the male's sperm within the female's body.

A pregnant woman is not a "pour-some-sperm, then heat" crock pot!

Misogyny and sexism have painted females as "delicate and weak." Ha! Ever create a human being in your body, then deliver it to the world from a small opening? How about the 10+ babies from mothers of yore — and still today? *Oh, such weakness!*

Don't people realize, in horror, King Henry VIII (among others) actually had the head of his wife *chopped off?* He was upset her latest pregnancy produced a girl. Realize that now, science shows it is the **male** who **determines the gender** of a child.

Henry, if a male is so important, it should have been *your* head. Just sayin', Big Guy.

Will the many, many good and genuinely strong males in the world *please* **display outrage over misogyny and sexism? Despite progress in many areas, those cruelties are still alive and as serious as ever, in one form or another.**

CHAPTER 6: THE DANGERS OF A MISDIAGNOSIS

Listed below are Eye-Opening and sometimes Jaw-Dropping books and other scholarly reporting about how females have long been, and continue to be, regarded by the world—and by the medical profession, in particular:

BOOKS
- *How Doctors Think*, by Jerome Groopman, M.D.
- *All In Her Head*, by Elizabeth Comen, M.D.
- *Endometriosis: The Doctor Will See You Now*, by Tamer Seckin, M.D.
- *Invisible Women: Data Bias in a World Designed for Men*, by Caroline Criado Perez
- *Delusions of Gender*, by Cordelia Fine
- *The Man They Wanted Me to Be: Toxic Masculinity*, by Jared Yates Sexton
- *A Taste of My Own Medicine*, by Dr. Edward E. Rosenbaum
- *Inferior: How Science Got Women Wrong*, by Angela Saini
- *Womb/The Inside Story of Where We All Began*, by Leah Hazard
- *Doing Harm*, by Maya Dusenbery
- *Unwell Women/Diagnosis and Myth in a Man-Made World*, by Elinor Cleghorn
- *Caste: The Origins of Our Discontents*, by Isabel Wilkerson
- *Sink,* by Joseph Earl Thomas

- *Healing Spiritual Wounds/Reconnecting with a Loving God After Experiencing a Hurtful Church*, by Carol Howard Merritt
- *Woman/The American History of an Idea*, by Lillian Faderman
- *Formidable: American Women and the Fight for Equality,* by Elisabeth Griffith
- *Vagina Obscura/An Anatomical Voyage*, by Rachel E. Gross
- *The Handmaid's Tale* and *The Testaments,* by Margaret Atwood
- *The Body Keeps the Score,* by Bessel van der Kolk, M.D.
- *What Happened to You?*, by Bruce D. Perry, M.D., Ph.D. and Oprah Winfrey

OTHER RESOURCES
- January 4, 2023 NPR Broadcast: "Why Are Women's Health Concerns Dismissed So Often?" Participants included:
  Dr. Raegan McDonald-Mosley, Practicing OB/GYN and CEO of Power to Decide; Anushay Hossain, author of *The Pain Gap: How Sexism and Racism in Healthcare Kill Women;* and Dr. Deirdre Cooper Owens, author of *Medical Bondage*

- August 15, 2023, Huffpost.com: "I Begged My Doctors To Figure Out What Was Wrong With Me. Instead, I Was Medically Gaslit," by Julie Strack

A VERIFIABLE
DIAGNOSIS
AT LAST

SURPRISE,
SURPRISE,
SURPRISE.

CHAPTER 6: THE DANGERS OF A MISDIAGNOSIS

Sometime between early 1974, when my physical problems began, and very late 1994/very early 1995, when my first **accurate** diagnosis arrived, I decided my problems were, indeed, psychogenic.

I believed my physical symptoms were actually occurring but resulted from emotional issues. And I decided the emotional issues stemmed from my gloomy feelings about being gay. No one specifically suggested this analysis, but it increasingly made sense to me. With increasing confidence, I thought: *No more denial* from me. Needing a shrink has won. I need to find a way to make peace with myself and I'm eager to accomplish this journey.

I tossed my enduring belief aside: I do *not* have Multiple Sclerosis. ***Goodbye, MS!***

Then I learned this:

***"Not So Fast,"* and**
"You've Gotta Be Kidding."
Sometimes we're smarter than we know.

A verifiable truth had arrived.
And I knew just what to say:

Hello, MS.
I really always knew it was you.
We've been together for a long time.

CHAPTER 7

1994/1995

DR. CATHLEEN E. SCHMITT

SHE BELIEVES ME

CHAPTER 7: DOCTORS BELIEVE ME – 1994/1995

Isn't it interesting how answers sometimes arrive when we least expect them, when we've let our guard down—or even intentionally stopped wondering and looking? That's where my head and heart were in 1994, at age 43. That's also when my life would take a major shift, a jaw-dropping shift, on the second-to-last day of that year: the day before New Year's Eve, 1994.

The expression, *You could have knocked me over with a feather*, comes to mind.

My phone at work rang just as late afternoon on Friday, December 30, 1994, arrived. I was in a happy mood, looking forward to a New Year's Eve party the next day with friends. I'm not usually a big New Year's Eve partier, but Betty and I were looking forward to food and drinks with our friends Micheline and Jeff and to being at John and Sue's house on the 31st. It was always an interesting and fun time with all of them. I was surprised when my regular doctor, Cathleen Schmitt, identified herself when I picked up the phone. She herself never called me at work and I don't recall any of her staff members ever using my work number. But there she was. Maybe I shouldn't have been surprised. Both Dr. Schmitt and I were interested in learning the results of my first-ever MRI of my brain and spinal cord. Without exactly saying so, I knew she anticipated the revelation of some potentially serious disease. I was expecting nothing. Seriously. For more than twenty years, I had endured physical problems arriving and leaving—and often arriving and leaving again—in relentless episodes, and I always passed every medical test. I had endured the *nothing-is-wrong* and condescending dismissiveness from doctors for so long that I had given up. I decided to believe my problems were indeed psychosomatic, caused by deep distress over being gay. I worked that idea into my emotional comfort zone. Seemed plausible enough, plus—**plus**—I wanted to get doctors—male doctors—out of my life, forever and ever, amen. *You don't get to hurt me, to try to brainwash me, ever again.*

Did I really, deeply, believe my twenty-plus-year health nightmare was psychosomatic? No. **No.**

But I can honestly say I wasn't expecting Dr. Schmitt's message. I had truly given up, and that felt more comfortable—psychologically safer—than for me to try to pursue the truth again. Learning I had a serious disease *wasn't* psychologically threatening; being negated and patronized by male doctors had increasingly become my terror. It took all my strength and determination just to handle my physical problems. Then I also had to find more strength and energy to pursue my career ambitions in a sexist and misogynistic world. All of that effort might have been somewhat mitigated if I were attracted to males and

CHAPTER 7: DOCTORS BELIEVE ME – 1994/1995

happily, delightedly, dating them. But just knowing I was gay, with all that could mean, especially in that era, further dragged me down psychologically. It was all just too much. So I was no longer going to let medical men drag me down even further. What an irony and tragedy, I often thought. Doctors are supposed to commit to "First Do No Harm." Ha! My experience had taught me: *Stay away from male doctors. They harm you. Run like the wind from them!*

In fact, that was why a *female* doctor was calling me. I'd stopped seeing specialists or any other type of doctor for my supposedly mysterious or psychosomatic malady. I vowed to myself I would only tell any new doctor about my health saga if it seemed of critical importance. And I wanted as many of my doctors as possible to be female. Dr. Cathleen Schmitt knew **nothing** about my twenty-year health situation. She was my doctor for the likes of an ear or sinus infection. I didn't want to risk her pegging me as a weirdo, whiner, or hypochondriac if I told her about the "MS symptoms" that specialists and other doctors had tested and ruled out. Never, *never*, would I take that risk again unless my condition seemed to cry out for it.

But the day came a few months earlier in 1994 when I suddenly got vertigo. It took nearly two months for the dizziness to resolve, despite the treatment prescribed by Dr. Schmitt for this surmised inner-ear infection. Then, in the immediate aftermath of its resolution, my left leg began buckling in such a strange and unpredictable way. I nearly fell several times because my left leg seemed not to be working too well all of a sudden. Was it numb? Then the leg would sometimes bend and lurch upward and then return to normal after I slowly counted to ten. Just so weird — it had the markings of my "MS stuff." Damn. Here we go again.

So, I decided to tell Dr. Schmitt about the leg buckling — this, on top of her recent help with the vertigo. But I didn't breathe a word about the twenty-year symptoms. I didn't mention MS. She knew nothing about all those other doctors or their tests or their leading me towards the psychiatrist Dr. Bland. So, imagine my thoughts and feelings when Dr. Cathleen E. Schmitt looked at me with the utmost seriousness and declared, "I'm going to order an MRI of your brain and spinal cord."

"Oh, Dr. Schmitt, I don't need an MRI," I responded. "I've never had one, but there's a whole history I've never told you about. I've had years and years of on and off physical problems. Weird skin sensations, eye troubles, all sorts of things. I've seen many doctors and I pass all their tests. They don't know what's wrong or they say or imply it's a mental health issue.

CHAPTER 7: DOCTORS BELIEVE ME – 1994/1995

I saw a psychiatrist for a few years. I got a little better, but then new symptoms cropped up or old ones came back. I just need a new shrink."

Our eyes locked. Her eyes seemed to bore into me.

"I'll order that MRI right away." Our eyes continued to lock.

"Okay." I kept looking at Dr. Schmitt. I didn't want our connection to break.

I started to feel kind of strange, but a good strange.

As I drove home, I almost felt tranquilized, at peace.

There is nothing like being believed.

So now it's December 30, 1994, and Dr. Cathleen E. Schmitt is calling me.

She apologized for calling me at work, but explained my MRI results had just come in. She realized it was late Friday afternoon, the day before New Year's Eve. She wanted to catch me in case I had big partying plans; I might want to proceed with caution now.

Her voice was gentle. She told me the radiologist praised my description of the symptoms I'd experienced throughout the past twenty years. He said they guided him as he evaluated my MRI results. Dr. Schmitt continued. The MRI showed numerous "lesions" in my brain, especially in the cerebellum. The lesions, combined with all my symptoms now and over the years, suggested a diagnosis of Multiple Sclerosis, or MS, as it's usually called. I started to cry.

Dr. Schmitt attempted to comfort me until I gently stopped her. I told her I wasn't crying because I might have MS; I was crying because doctor after doctor over the past twenty years told me I did *not* have MS or any other medical disease. I said I *thought* I had MS after researching diseases in medical books at a bookstore in 1974—**1974**—because **doctors** weren't taking me seriously. But my doctors—including a team of **neurologists** at a large and well-regarded hospital—said I didn't have MS. They suggested psychological treatment. Then my *psychiatrist* told me to stop talking about having MS because the medical community had ruled it out. The doctors patronized me and didn't guide me towards any other expertise than mental health. I was left to figure things out on my own. I finally gave up. They kind of brainwashed me, Dr. Schmitt! Remember I told you just a few days ago that I didn't need an MRI—that all I needed was more psychotherapy?

CHAPTER 7: DOCTORS BELIEVE ME – 1994/1995

I cried very little over the next few weeks. But I raged like a wild animal, a bear that was *so done* with being poked by men. I was raring and roaring to poke back. Good thing I'm not a physically aggressive woman (and most of those doctors were dead by then). **Hell Hath No Fury**....

When Dr. Schmitt said she would refer me to a male neurologist here in Marin County, California, Dr. James Kelly, I said I would vastly prefer a female neurologist—anywhere, if necessary, in the Bay Area. Dr. Schmitt assured me I would like and respect Dr. Kelly. *She was so right.* Thank you again, Dr. Schmitt (and Dr. Kelly). Dr. James Kelly turned out to be a blessing in my life, and so medically and psychologically critical to me at this juncture. He radiated kindness, intelligence, and knowledge. He treated me with obvious respect and deep caring. **He** not only **listened**, he also **asked my opinion** and **complimented me**. It was as if I'd suddenly turned into a very wise and brave patient.

I remember my psychiatrist, Dr. Bland, commenting in 1976 about how easily I recited my seven or so physical problems to him. I did a double-take: was that just a comment, or was he praising me, OR did I hear a touch of negativity—as in maybe I'm too focused on my health, hypochondriac-style? I asked him what he meant. Of course, "Dr. Freudian" didn't respond. So, I responded. I said it took little effort to remember seven distinct physical issues that had been a part of my life on and off for several years, especially since I was trying so hard to describe them with precision to various types of doctors in order to effect an accurate diagnosis and treatment plan. Of course, he said nothing.

Scary as any diagnosis of MS can be, I knew enough about the disease in 1994-1995 to know I had a more "benign" form of it. It seemed unlikely that I would face anything close to what the delightful actress Annette Funicello was facing. My generation just loved her in her "Beach Party" movies with Frankie Avalon, among others. It was staggeringly sad to read that her "Primary Progressive" form of MS was relentlessly crippling her (and, ultimately, shortening and taking her life).

I was not crippled at all after twenty years, so that helped me stay pretty calm about my new official diagnosis of "*Probable* Relapsing/Remitting Multiple Sclerosis." I now had hard evidence from magnetic resonance brain and spinal cord imaging that I had nerve damage in my central nervous system. MS *lesions* (scars or plaques) were showing in different parts of my brain. The myelin sheath, the important fatty covering of nerves, was being attacked by my immune system as if it were a foreign enemy. This

CHAPTER 7: DOCTORS BELIEVE ME – 1994/1995

type of tragic confusion is found in autoimmune diseases. I found the truth upsetting, but also felt relieved by solid answers and genuinely caring doctors.

My diagnosis was, of course, very troubling for my family members and friends. Betty was bravely and lovingly at my side. Mom flew down from Humboldt County and spent several days with us. She brought bags of various B vitamins and other recommended treatments from the local health store. I know the thought of my potentially becoming crippled devastated her and my father. They were almost frantically trying to help. She told me my older sister Cathy had let out a scream at her workplace when she heard my diagnosis. Bless their hearts. I tried to reassure everyone my doctors didn't think I was likely to become seriously impaired.

I didn't quite dare to ask Dr. Kelly if he'd like to see my own notes or the materials from previous doctors. *I have perceptions of psychiatrist Dr. Bland in my head*: don't come across as a hypochondriac, as too immersed in health issues. But I did dare to ask his nurse. I loved her response: "I think he'll appreciate it!"

So, I dropped a newly dusted off manila folder at Dr. Kelly's office a few days later. At my next appointment,

Dr. Kelly said, "Oh, Jenny, your information is so helpful." He sighed. "If only my other patients would do this."

"If only my other patients would do this."

Maybe I want that as my epitaph.

My diagnosis of "Probable MS" in early 1995 would turn into two other diagnoses as my disease slowly progressed over the years. Dr. Kelly eventually retired, but I saw other excellent neurologists both in Marin County and in San Francisco. One of them included Dr. Douglas Goodin, referred to as an "internationally renowned MS specialist" practicing at UCSF (the University of California at San Francisco includes a topnotch hospital with a highly regarded neurology department). He confirmed Dr. Kelly's findings and added more testing. My Evoked Potentials showed slowed responses (nerve damage) in my right eye and left leg.

Dr. Kelly had also demonstrated that I had "Lhermitte's Sign" — a feeling of electrical shocks went down my back and arms when I looked down sharply. I'd never noticed it before. I seldom feel it now, but it's a sign of nerve damage. Then my left leg suddenly went numb, and the numbness crept up my left side to just under my breast. It resolved after about six weeks.

CHAPTER 7: DOCTORS BELIEVE ME – 1994/1995

Dr. Kelly (among later neurologists and ophthalmologists) believed my "Central Serous Retinopathy" diagnosis by an ophthalmologist in 1985 was more likely a case of "Optic Neuritis." I had suddenly developed color perception problems (first in my left eye, then the right) in 1985. Red, black, and yellow colors were now faded, and I eventually developed a blind spot in the center of the left eye. It all resolved (thank heavens) after about six months. The original eye specialist had ordered the recommended diagnostic dye testing of my eyes. He said my results corresponded with Central Serous Retinopathy (CSR), a potentially sight-threatening condition. Gulp. He said my condition was caused by stress. CSR and Optic Neuritis are similar and are sometimes confused with one another, resulting in a misdiagnosis. Optic Neuritis is common in MS patients (sometimes their first symptom), and the pallor ophthalmologists now see in one of my optic nerves seems a telltale sign of the nerve damage from that condition.

Fortunately, I can find humor in many otherwise anger- and cynicism-producing situations. It helps to laugh. I've always had a huge fear of blindness, so you can imagine my reaction when the ophthalmologist in 1985 told me I could go blind if I didn't reduce my stress. Here's an indicator of how seriously I responded to this doctor (let's call him *Dr. Blind*): it took me almost three **years** to decide to go to a mental health practitioner (Dr. Bland) when I first came down with my mysterious physical problems, but I selected a psychologist and was sitting in her office three **days** after my diagnosis from Dr. Blind. With my permission, my new psychologist conferred with Dr. Blind. He counseled her to use a substantial part of my therapy hour each week undergoing relaxation/stress reduction techniques with her.

Now, it's usually good for people not to be too stressed out. You and I can see why stress reduction work could be really good for those who actually suffer from something like Central Serous Retinopathy (CSR) because stress is causing their possible blindness. Right? But what if you don't actually have that disease with that cause? What if years after all those relaxation sessions had cut into your weekly talk therapy sessions (and all the money you spent), you learn you never had *CSR caused by stress*! You learn you actually had *optic nerve damage caused by Optic Neuritis from MS*! My optic nerves were inflamed and scarred by the autoimmune attacks of Multiple Sclerosis. *Oops.*

So now this eye condition "Oops" has been added to the overall **Great Big Oops** — you know the big one:

"Jenny, you do not have MS."

CHAPTER 7: DOCTORS BELIEVE ME – 1994/1995

"Jenny, you do not have a medical disease;"

"Jenny, your problems are *functional*. Perhaps you should seek mental health counseling;"

"Jenny, you suffer from Anxiety Neurosis with a Psycho-Physiological Reaction of the Neuro-Musculo-Skeletal System;"

"Jenny, to get better, you need to take a serious look at yourself."

Thanks, Docs!

Do doctors ever realize patients actually "own" their diseases? Their diseases reside within their bodies, often for a very long time. That tends to cause acute knowledge of the disease process and details. Ask us, Doctors. Please listen. Trust us. Respect our insights and opinions.

MS and I have lived together for 50 years. I'm still standing and moving. People are stunned to hear I have the disease.

But some significant changes are here, and others seem to be on the horizon.

I went from my initial official diagnosis of "Probable" Relapsing/Remitting MS in early 1995—twenty-one years after my symptoms began in early 1974—to "Definite" Relapsing/Remitting MS sometime in the late 1990s. Bit by bit, as the years passed, I got more physical problems, underwent more MRI scans, and developed more brain and spine lesions, including "black holes" that indicate permanent brain damage.

My neurologists and I had decided *not* to start me on any of the few MS medications in existence in the 1990s because they only increased the time in between "exacerbations"—when symptoms cropped up again. We felt my body handled that well, all by itself. As the years went by, my most hated symptom, Crawling Sensations of the Skin, had settled way, way down to non-existent (my gratitude knows no bounds). This seems to indicate the inflammation that causes myelin to burn off had completed its task, allowing some skin sensations to dwindle. But now, while my skin *felt* better to me, the resulting nerve damage sometimes caused nerve signals to go haywire. Some effects of seemingly permanent nerve damage had arrived; others lurked.

Many of my friends and co-workers over the next 25 years (1997-2022) didn't even know I had MS. I was not at all crippled (most people with MS don't become crippled), I virtually never got sick (no sick

CHAPTER 7: DOCTORS BELIEVE ME – 1994/1995

days in 18 years at my final job before retirement in 2017), and I preferred the whole discussion of MS to drift into quiet, private land. Privacy sometimes became easier with a disease like Multiple Sclerosis because certain "exacerbations" could be attributed to other ailments (or may have indeed resulted from other ailments). I intentionally attributed a condition I developed around 2003 to something other than MS. It was easier professionally to do so—and who knows why I got it?

The "it" is Bell's palsy.

Bell's palsy results from an inflammation or disruption of a facial nerve. The cause is unknown. Anyone can be its victim, but it's also the first symptom of MS for some people. Bell's palsy is very scary until you know how your suddenly partially "melted face" is going to end up. My family knew a man whose face seemed to take forever to return to (almost) normal and a female friend whose face never recovered. Nothing prepares you to look in the mirror and find half your face is drooping. I gasped when I saw myself. Is it a stroke? Bell's palsy? Fortunately, my new female Marin neurologist, Dr. Ilkcan Cokgor, prescribed prednisone, and I was **way** better after six weeks. It completely resolved not long after. Phew.

As the early 2000s merged into the teens, I began experiencing a different type of MS problem. These symptoms seemed more dangerous, as though they might be precursors of some kind of permanent impairment. The worst happened in 2014. I was simply taking a bath in my bathtub—something I often preferred to a shower. I luxuriated in the warmth of the water. Now, it was simply time to get out of the tub. How many times had I done this over the course of my life? But this time (at age 63), after unplugging and watching the water go down the drain, I couldn't get out. Not because I was "gettin' old and out of shape" but because all of a sudden my hands and feet didn't work. They flopped around. There was no muscle tone. I couldn't push down on them for traction and support. Terrified, I screamed for Betty. Alarmed and unable to make sense of what was happening, she grabbed a phone to call 911. I told her, **No**. Even though I'd never experienced anything like this, I just knew it was MS calling. I had read there was something about MS and warmth that could be bad. "We just need to haul me out of the tub. When I cool down, I bet my hands and feet will go back to normal." Betty was understandably skeptical as well as scared. We argued. No 911 for now! We slowly got me out of the tub and onto the cool bathroom floor. As I thought, I quite quickly got somewhat better. The floor was uncomfortable, so I crawled on my forearms and knees to the nearby

CHAPTER 7: DOCTORS BELIEVE ME – 1994/1995

living room rug and then eventually rolled myself onto the couch. More comfortable—and I was cooling down, cooling down. After a while (was it a half hour?), my hands and feet were seemingly back to normal. It felt like those body parts had now reawakened, had "come alive." Talk about frightening. Talk about weird. Talk about MS.

I have never taken a *bath* since that day. I only take relatively short *showers*.

My current neurologist, Dr. Lynda Lam, said my perceptions of what was happening in the bathtub that day in 2014 were correct. She added that one of the past (prior to the development of MRIs) diagnostic tools for MS involved immersing patients in warm water. MS symptoms often got worse.

The other thing I started to develop around 2014 (on and off) was a feeling of **very heavy legs.** It felt as if I wore heavy metal braces on my legs or big bags of sand were suddenly attached to them. Once, I was wrapping Christmas presents on the living room rug and needed to jump up to get the phone. This was increasingly difficult. Sometimes, the difficulty pointed to being older and out of shape. But other times, the culprit was the inexplicable periodic return of the heavy legs. It seemed even an Olympian would struggle getting up. My legs didn't look any different, but something was certainly going on. (Hint: nerve damage.) Between that and my continuous concern about the 2014 bathtub event, I knew I should call Dr. Lam.

It was now December 2020. I suggested setting up another MRI in, say, January. Dr. Lam immediately ordered one—for December.

I expected to learn I had a worsening case of Relapsing/Remitting MS and that we'd decide to start me on one of the newish immunosuppressive drugs. All good, I thought. In fact, how lucky am I! Twenty-five years have gone by since my first MS diagnosis and at last there are more promising medications. No cures, but new drugs that slow MS progression. And since my case moves slowly, what perfect timing! My disease process seems to have come full circle, I said to myself. The new medication should tie it all up in a nice bow!

Ah, no, Jenny.

The latest MRI results were devastating. I didn't see them coming.

"Secondary Progressive Multiple Sclerosis, in a Moderate-to-Severe Range."

CHAPTER 7: DOCTORS BELIEVE ME – 1994/1995

"Progressive" is part of the diagnosis, a diagnosis approaching **Severe**. *NO!*

I called Betty from Dr. Lam's parking lot. We cried. **Oh, No....**

I wanted to scream from every rooftop. I wanted to pound all those early doctors for their stupidity, negation, and lack of belief in what I described so well to them. "You don't have MS or any medical disease, Jenny." *Right, Guys!* **I figured it out** by going to a bookstore on my lunch hour **in 1974**. I paid attention to the details. I believed me. Dr. Bland, the psychiatrist, even suggested *psychoanalysis* when I wasn't improving enough. Thank God I didn't waste time and money on that.

My mind raced through all the psychological therapy I'd forced myself to go through on and off for years with several different therapists. Tears flowed, remembering the day I excitedly showed my family members the new biography of Senator Edmund Muskie. *The Senate Nobody Knows* contained a tribute to me. Doubleday had assigned author Bernard Asbell to write a book about the U.S. Senate through examining the work of Senator Muskie and his staff. I just happened to have started the receptionist part of my job on Senator Muskie's staff by 1975 when Bernie began his research. He practically lived in our office for months. I was thrilled with his characterization: The reception room was *"made warm and lively by Jenny Wood, a long-tressed, dark-eyed woman in her early twenties, who has the unmistakable air of 'good family,' and a talent for welcoming not visitors but persons."* My family expressed their pride and joy, too. Then someone piped up: "A good family, but you have to see a *psychiatrist.*"

Those words still sting. They certainly shouldn't have been said, at least *not* to me. But they also reflected how families and businesses and society at large back then commonly regarded "mental health" issues and the kind of people who had them. I had to fight my own prejudices and stereotyping in order to seek and receive such treatment. It can be so helpful. Many of us, myself included, have a much more enlightened and compassionate understanding now. Nonetheless, here I was in 2021, trying to digest my newest official diagnosis, when Bernie Asbell's wonderful book suddenly came to mind. I thought about my years and years of therapy, the primary aim of which was to find and fix the source of my physical problems. I thought about all the years my family had worried about me, with the psychological/psychiatric element presenting a different kind of anxiety for all of us. I had made the decision to select a **psychiatrist** as my first therapist because I wanted a ***medical doctor*** as my mental health professional, even though I knew

CHAPTER 7: DOCTORS BELIEVE ME – 1994/1995

seeing a "psychiatrist" held even more threatening connotations in society in that era. That decision seemed to especially bother my otherwise very loving family member.

Funny how that long-ago comment suddenly struck me as I was absorbing the facts about my seriously worsening condition. I'd not thought about the comment in years. It reemerged as I learned anew I'd suffered from Multiple Sclerosis all along. All along. Maybe my thought process was beaming some kind of release from all the suffering my family and I had endured. I was damn proud to have been right all along about MS. I was also relieved (even more than I initially realized) to be released from, "What's wrong with Jenny?"

But I also knew this about **progressive** MS: I had entered the land of potential canes and walkers and wheelchairs — and not because of old age. The land of potential cognitive decline, blindness, swallowing problems, and other types of bodily destruction.

I had had to fight so hard all those years just to be believed that it never really, deeply, sank in that I might one day experience the frightening, heartbreaking decline of someone like Annette Funicello.

Was that foolish of me? I don't think so. I had to save my energy just to get through my days with what was clearly before me — all those physical problems and the demeaning responses of my doctors.

Doctors **harmed** me psychologically. This had lasted my whole adulthood, from age 22 on. I was so exhausted.

CHAPTER 8

2021:

SECONDARY PROGRESSIVE MULTIPLE SCLEROSIS, MODERATE-TO-SEVERE RANGE

OH NO!

CHAPTER 8: I TOLD YOU I HAD MS – 2021

Through tears, I sat in my car outside Dr. Lam's office and thought carefully about her reassuring words, as well as the MS information I knew or had just Googled:

- Most people with Multiple Sclerosis have **Relapsing/Remitting MS.** Most cases begin between ages 20 to 40.

- About 10 to 15 years after that initial diagnosis, most patients are diagnosed with **Secondary Progressive MS** (meaning, in the first part, symptoms come and sometimes go and sometimes return, but now, in the second part, symptoms stay and may get progressively, but unpredictably, worse).

- I am *now* where those first diagnosed with **Primary Progressive MS** (such as actress Annette Funicello) *begin*. New symptoms are now predicted to remain or worsen. (No more relapsing and remitting.)

- I was fortunate to maintain a relapsing/remitting status for over 40 years.

- There are now promising medications that suppress a patient's immune system. **Multiple Sclerosis is an autoimmune disease**, meaning that for some reason, a patient's body can't tell the difference between a foreign cell and the patient's own cells. In MS, this results in an immune system that attacks the myelin sheath protectively covering the patient's nerves—as if the myelin sheath is an enemy. Immunosuppressive drugs aim to stop this.

- Dr. Lam strongly recommended I begin infusions of the immunosuppressant Rituximab (trade name Rituxan). Given my age (70 when starting treatment) and other factors, she felt this drug offered my best chance of slowing MS progression. Rituximab, a monoclonal antibody medication, is showing impressive results in improving the health status of patients suffering from several diseases, such as Rheumatoid Arthritis and Non-Hodgkin's Lymphoma (the disease that ended Jacqueline Kennedy's life), as well as MS.

- Dr. Lam believes I won't ever become impaired to the point of needing a wheelchair (especially after receiving these treatments).

- Increasing evidence that the **Epstein-Barr virus** is a leading cause of MS may lead to new treatments or even a cure for MS.

Reviewing all this information did comfort me. I discussed Rituximab with Betty and the rest of my family. I said Yes to Rituximab infusions, which started in 2021 and now receive every six months. The process is easy, and I have no side effects. Kudos to my Infusion Center. The nurses are wonderful. The setting is full of sunlight and offers as much privacy as one might like. I relax and read and write during this four-to-six-hour process. (I don't mind my infusions at all.) **Go Rituximab!**

I TOLD YOU I HAD MS

CHAPTER 9

HOW DOCTORS MIGHT IMPROVE THEIR DIAGNOSTIC PROCESS AND COMMUNICATIONS WITH THEIR PATIENTS

Sometimes, say and suggest just a little bit more. The "a little bit more" can make a significant difference.

How about something like this?
(with adjustments, given different issues)

"Jenny, I've ordered all the tests that relate to your symptoms as you describe them and from my evaluations. As you know, you've passed all of them. And that's great!

"I know you're still concerned because your symptoms haven't fully subsided yet. Sometimes it can take a while for our systems to settle down after we've been stressed, wondering if there is something seriously wrong.

"I recommend you try as best you can right now to relax, knowing you've passed all these important tests. Try to get some exercise, eat well, and get restful sleep.

If your symptoms still don't settle down after a period of time, there are **specialists** in a variety of fields, such as neurology and endocrinology, you might want to consult. My opinion is these specialists will also not find anything seriously wrong, but I want you to know these specialties exist **and I'll be happy to refer you to them if desired.**

"Some patients ask if they should seek *mental and emotional health evaluations* when months and months of unexplained physical problems persist. That's also something you might want to explore should this happen. *Sometimes* this is a good idea because **it turns out there *is* a mental or emotional health issue that needs attention. Other times, a counselor can provide comfort and guidance to patients coping with a variety of health issues.**

"Right now, though, I recommend you try to relax, feel good about all the tests you passed, and then remember there are these other areas to pursue, if you desire."

(Comprehensive, helpful, supportive, respectful. Right?)

DO THE BEST YOU CAN
UNTIL YOU KNOW BETTER.

THEN WHEN YOU KNOW BETTER,
DO BETTER.

Maya Angelou

LET'S TAKE A BREAK FROM SERIOUS TOPICS!

REMEMBER
I TOLD YOU TOWARDS THE
BEGINNING OF THE BOOK
I WANTED TO
SAVE THE BEST FOR LAST?

WE'VE ARRIVED.

LET'S START BY DRIFTING BACK
IN TIME,
TO 1978 AND TO 1979...

LIFE CAN DISH OUT A LOT OF
DIFFICULTY.

BUT HERE'S TO
THE MAGIC
LIFE CAN ALSO PROVIDE.

DON'T
EVER
FORGET THE MAGIC!

CHAPTER 10

DREAMS COME TRUE

HYANNIS PORT, MASSACHUSETTS, 1978

THE KENNEDYS
AND
THE SALINGERS

THE WEEKEND IT ALL HAPPENED

August 1978

CHAPTER 10: DREAMS COME TRUE

As the title of this book indicates, numerous challenges arrived in my young adulthood that then required decades of facing and fighting various forms of adversity. I refused to be derailed or slowed as I raced after my exciting ambitions. Wondrous dreams started to come true. Sometimes dreams I didn't quite dare to dream came true. Come along with me and see what I mean.

What I'm now going to describe happened one weekend in August of 1978 in Hyannis Port, Massachusetts, at the Kennedy Compound on Cape Cod. This setting comprised President John F. Kennedy's "Summer White House." I was 27.

**I was a guest at the Kennedy Compound.
I was a *guest* of Ethel (Mrs. Robert) Kennedy.**

My wildest dreams came true that weekend.

This book is in part dedicated to Suzanne Salinger, the daughter of President Kennedy's Press Secretary Pierre Salinger, because she brought me to the setting of this dream (and several others). *The Kennedy family took it the rest of the way.*

Why don't I refresh your memory of earlier chapters where I discuss Pierre Salinger and how I met his daughter Suzanne?

Even if you're not a fan of the Kennedys, I think you might enjoy this adventure.

I still can't quite believe it happened, but it is true. My 12-year-old self is smiling.

It was my luckiest of all weekends.

THANK YOU, SUZANNE SALINGER

CHAPTER 10: DREAMS COME TRUE

Most Americans probably don't give much thought to who's serving as Press Secretary to the President of the United States. I mean, a couple of them in recent years have had less than stellar "performance" issues discussed in the news, but it seems most Americans don't pay much attention to the subject. Naturally, I always remembered Pierre Salinger as Press Secretary to President John F. Kennedy—because I remember almost everything Kennedy. I also happily recalled Pierre Salinger as a wise and charming personality—a "bon vivant" all by himself. But I'm sometimes surprised (and pleased) all these years later when people exclaim to me, "You actually *knew* Pierre Salinger? His daughter was a good friend of yours? He treated you two to dinner at Sans Souci in its heyday? You and Pierre Salinger's daughter spent a weekend at the Kennedy Compound in Hyannis Port? Tell me more!"

Well, okay.

Pierre Salinger came from his own noteworthy family. His maternal grandfather was elected to the French parliament and his mother, Jehanne Bietry Salinger, as described earlier, was an author and journalist in her own right. Pierre had had an impressive career and exhibited striking talents (he was a child piano prodigy) long before he met, first,

Robert F. Kennedy and then Robert's big brother, Senator John F. Kennedy.

Pierre's career, starting in 1947 as a shrewd and energetic investigative journalist for *The San Francisco Chronicle*, caught the eye of Robert Kennedy, then serving as counsel for the U.S. Senate Select Committee on Improper Activities in Labor and Management. Pierre left San Francisco for Washington, D.C. to work for the committee from 1957 to 1959. His contribution led to other appointments endorsed by both Kennedy brothers and to his becoming part of the Kennedy inner circle even before his days as Presidential Press Secretary.

Pierre Salinger's closeness to the Kennedy family remained long after both brothers were assassinated. He was often seen at Jacqueline Kennedy's side after 1963. Ten years after Robert Kennedy's death, Pierre's youngest child, Gregory, who otherwise lived in France, spent part of the summer of 1978 at the Kennedy Compound as a guest of RFK's widow, Ethel. Indeed, Ethel Kennedy had invited Suzanne Salinger (and thus me) to the Compound in order to spend time with her 11-year-old brother. (Gregory and Suzanne had different mothers.)

Let's just say, if one of my goals following President Kennedy's assassination was to get to know members

CHAPTER 10: DREAMS COME TRUE

of the Kennedy family and their inner circle, I received a sparkling prize when I met Pierre Salinger. And I didn't even have to work for it! Pierre and Suzanne bounced right into my arms—before I ever reached out.

Please recall from the beginning of this book that a family friend, Monsieur Gaspard Weiss, decided *on his own* to find a woman in Washington, D.C. who could look out for 21-year-old me if I needed any help during my maiden voyage to the nation's capital in 1973. Monsieur Weiss consulted his friend in Monterey, California, a friend named Jehanne Bietry Salinger-Carlson—Pierre's mother. Her letter of introduction led to my wonderful friendship with Barbara Gamarekian, who had served in the JFK White House Press Office headed by Pierre Salinger.

That's how Jenny met his daughter, Suzanne! Please recall: **No, it wasn't.** Completely by chance, I met Suzanne Salinger because of my terrible waitress job at a restaurant near the Mayflower Hotel in downtown Washington, D.C. in 1973. (The job was so bad, I quit after a week.) But remember the first customer I waited on (named Joe) my very first night? He simply asked me a few seemingly innocuous questions—nothing about the Kennedys or Salingers—and the next thing I hear him say to his friend, "Ed, we ought to introduce Jenny to

Suzanne." The next day, Suzanne nearly keeled over thinking her friend Joe had just met "a *cocktail waitress* who'd come to town from California with a *letter of recommendation*" from her grandmother, the very French author and journalist, Jehanne Bietry Salinger. "I just *have* to meet you," Suzanne said to me by phone with glee.

Suzanne and I "clicked" right away. We'd go in and out of each other's lives as either she or I moved here and there over the years, but we both landed back in D.C. in the 1977-80 period. And the day came in August of 1978 when she called and told me her brother was staying with the Robert Kennedy family at the Cape and Ethel Kennedy had invited her up. Would I like to join her for the upcoming weekend?

How do you guess I responded to her? Heck, how do you think **most** people would respond? But for me and my lifetime dream? This was the culmination of my resolve after President Kennedy's death.

Oh, Baby!

Of course, you could write this yourself!

Tears still fill my eyes reliving this moment.

CHAPTER 10: DREAMS COME TRUE

Even knowing Suzanne for five years, it never occurred to me we'd go to the Kennedy Compound together.

I just cherish this. It must be like opening an envelope and learning you've won the Biggest Lottery Ever. Ready?

I said **No**.

You heard me. I said **No**.

Thank you so much, but I really shouldn't.

No, I really can't.

What the Hell?

You see, I'd had two hospitalizations that summer. I'd suddenly developed an abscessed throat in June of 1978. It's known as a Peritonsillar Abscess. It hurts and is fairly serious. It required four days of intravenous antibiotics. Once a patient regains strength, the tonsils have to come out. So I had a tonsillectomy the next month, at the age of 27. I'd just gotten back to work and back to normalcy in Senator Muskie's office when Suzanne posed the question. I was nervous I wasn't fully up to my normal strength and might be overdoing things with air travel between D.C. and Boston and maybe sailing on the windswept seas by the Kennedy Compound…So I said…Unfortunately, No.

DID THEY TAKE YOUR BRAIN AND HEART OUT, ALONG WITH YOUR TONSILS?

No worries.

Five minutes after hanging up, I frantically called Suzanne back: "Is your offer still open?" "Of course." "I must have lost my mind for a moment! I don't care if I push the envelope. I'll be fine. Oh, My God, this is so wonderful. Thank you so much." Phew.

You can just imagine the reactions of my family, friends, and co-workers when I told them what I'd be doing over the coming weekend. Yeah, my little ol' weekend plans.

Please join me now in reliving the most spectacular weekend of my *entire* life.

It's a Saturday in August 1978. I'll be meeting Suzanne in the early morning at nearby National Airport, and we'll fly up to Logan Airport in Boston. It's a sunny day.

CHAPTER 10: DREAMS COME TRUE

I'll rent a car after we land—just by (very lucky) chance, a *large* sedan. I'll drive. Turns out, it's a very easy drive from Logan Airport to Hyannis. Depending on traffic, under two hours.

I'd been to Hyannis Port a couple of times before—with my uncle Jim (Mom's younger brother), his wife Jo Ann, and their daughter, my little cousin Ellen. They lived about an hour away in Hingham and also loved the Kennedys. As tourists, we'd walk as close as possible to the Compound, which was comprised of three Kennedy houses. We'd smile at the guard posted outside the private driveway. ***This day would be different***. This day, I was not a tourist but a **Kennedy guest**.

I paused the car by the friendly guard. Suzanne talked to him. He was expecting us *(expecting us!)* and directed me towards the very nearby Robert and Ethel Kennedy house. The John and Jacqueline Kennedy house was just behind theirs. The famous Big House where President Kennedy and his eight siblings and parents lived during summers as they grew up and which served as his Summer White House was visible from the RFK home where we were staying. I didn't see her, but was told the family matriarch, Rose Kennedy, was there that weekend.

Suzanne had mentioned to me we might spend the night with a friend who lived on nearby Martha's Vineyard. However, when Ethel Kennedy's assistant, Catherine, greeted us at the house door and asked if we'd be spending the night, I piped up, "Yes, thank you." I turned to Suzanne and sheepishly whispered, "That kind of popped out. Sorry—is it okay?" She smiled a knowing smile and said, Of course. (Thanks, Suzanne.) Catherine showed us to our pretty bedroom with twin beds and decorated with pictures of Robert Kennedy. Catherine said she'd accompany us to the spot where Mrs. Kennedy, Gregory Salinger, and other Kennedy and Shriver children had moored their sailboat. Next thing I knew, I was driving through the streets of Hyannis Port, Suzanne and Catherine in tow.

How was I feeling? Good. Damn good.

We found the boat easily. Ethel and numerous young Kennedys were waiting for us. *(Waiting for us!)* After greetings, several of the children of Robert and Ethel Kennedy, as well as the son of Eunice Kennedy Shriver—sister of John and Robert Kennedy—and two Kennedy dogs decided to jump into the large sedan, joining Suzanne and Greg Salinger, Catherine, and me on our drive back to the RFK house at the Kennedy Compound. I continued to be the driver. Squished next to me were Suzanne Salinger, with

CHAPTER 10: DREAMS COME TRUE

Ethel and RFK daughter Courtney on her lap, and then family aide Catherine compressed beside them. The two Kennedy dogs, lively in the back, were joined by Chris and Max Kennedy (Ethel & RFK sons), Anthony Shriver (son of Eunice Kennedy and Sargent Shriver), and Gregory Salinger. So, I would be driving three Kennedys, one Kennedy-Shriver, two Salingers, two Kennedy dogs, and aide Catherine through the streets of Hyannis and Hyannis Port. *Just try to imagine my thoughts.*

- OMG, OMG, OMG — is this really happening?

- Careful, Careful, Careful! Do NOT get into an accident.

- Then, reverberating through every part of me, the wonderful Linda Clifford song — *"If My Friends Could See Me Now!"*

When we got back to the house, I walked upstairs to the bedroom. There, sitting on the bed, was my purse. I'd left it there in all the excitement. So, I'd been driving without my license….

Ethel Kennedy and the others on the boat soon arrived, as well as other Kennedy children who hadn't gone sailing that day, plus other houseguests. Kennedy friend and nationally renowned journalist and news anchor, Roger Mudd, and his wife were among them. David Kennedy, Ethel and RFK's 23-year-old son, suddenly appeared. I heard Ethel say, "Oh, David, you're so thin!" I would later learn David was battling drug addiction.

Despite all my glorious feelings, I was increasingly panic-stricken Suzanne and I would be expected to play Touch Football on the sprawling lawns of the Compound. Touch Football was a favorite Kennedy family sport during JFK's and RFK's youths and was carried on with much publicity by the RFK clan. We'd heard houseguests were expected to play, too. Saying I'm not a good athlete is a gross understatement. My high *academic* achievements were unfortunately conjoined with a dismal display in high school and college sports. I got the lowest scores of all girls in my high school on the California Physical Education Tests—Poor in all categories—push-ups, sit-ups, climbing the rope, etc. Someone once asked me, "How is it even possible to get Poor in every category?" I gave her an appropriate response: "I found it very easy. I was a natural!" My friend, who is a nurse, hearing about my sad showing in physical education, recently suggested—I think even somewhat seriously—I might have had nerve-damaging Multiple Sclerosis my **whole life**. I said, *Yes! Let's run with that!* I joke, but it's a sore subject for me. Lots of humiliation. (And you can bet I wasn't

CHAPTER 10: DREAMS COME TRUE

going to attempt Touch Football at the Kennedy Compound!) Fortunately, the subject never came up.

The dinner hour was approaching, which meant the cocktail hour was afoot. I walked around the first floor of the house with my gin & tonic. I loved the green and pink colors adorning the rooms. They added warmth as well as pizzazz. I found the house lovely, very comfortable and appealing.

I smiled and said hello to Rory, the youngest of the eleven children of RFK and Ethel, reading in a nearby chair. Rory was born six months after Robert Kennedy's death. She was now almost ten. Amazing.

I looked out the front windows at the beautiful lawns and sparkling sea below, scenes that enthralled the whole world in pictures and videos of the Kennedy Compound. Everything was right in front of me. *I'm inside the house seeing all of this.* I thought about my resolve at age 12, the day after President Kennedy was killed, to bring my life into the Kennedy's orbit. Now, here I was with my actual *friend, Pierre Salinger's daughter*. I thought about the odds of how Suzanne and I met. It was all so staggeringly wonderful. You know what else I thought?

I KNEW THIS WOULD HAPPEN.
I KNEW IT. I JUST KNEW IT.

And that is the truth. It's different from saying you set lofty goals and worked hard to meet them. Or you had burning ambitions that ached to be achieved, so you damn well made sure you succeeded. Those statements portray parts of it, but not the essence of what I'm trying to convey. What I'm trying to say is found in a statement I made earlier in the book when describing how I would not let my illness, my pathetically treated malady from age 22 on, nor its dreadful symptoms, keep me from realizing my dreams. A sensation of bugs crawling on my shoulders, back, and face, having double vision? Doctors who belittled me? *Whatever* — just try to stop me. *Wild horses would fail.* I think this resolve stemmed from my somehow **knowing** my day would come. I could somehow feel it. And ridiculous as it may sound to some, there was something about the Kennedys that deeply drew me to them. I wasn't blind to their faults. I just knew we had some kind of *chemistry* that propelled me.

And so, a deeply happy smile came over me as I gazed at the gorgeous sea, Rose Kennedy in the Big House next door. The past five years — 1973 to 1978 — had been both extraordinarily good and extraordinarily bad. And I'd now landed inside the Kennedy Compound, where I was about to have dinner and spend the night. I was very excited, but also deeply contented. *I had arrived.*

CHAPTER 10: DREAMS COME TRUE

Someone called out for us to gather for dinner in the dining room. Ethel Kennedy and six of her eleven children ate with Suzanne and Gregory Salinger, Roger Mudd and his wife, and me that night. The Ethel and RFK children that night included David, Courtney, Chris, Max, Doug, and Rory. We had the choice of steak or lobster. I love lobster, but chose steak that night. The whole dinner was delicious and conversations easily flowed.

After dinner, David Kennedy approached Suzanne and me and asked if we'd like to join him and his friend for drinks at a local bar. *Well, Yes.* Next thing I knew, we were at a nice, lively place, probably in downtown Hyannis. David asked what I'd like to drink and got me a gin & tonic. I remember telling him how much I admired his father and that I'd worked on his presidential campaign in my hometown in Humboldt County, California. I said I was thrilled when his father actually came to little Arcata during the campaign. (I didn't mention, but will always remember that at one point, Robert Kennedy *held both* of my outstretched hands while smiling so warmly at me. I so wish I had a picture of it. He was assassinated three weeks later, just before my high school graduation in 1968.)

I periodically looked at David and Suzanne as we sat at our table talking and laughing away. *Bobby*

Kennedy's son. Pierre Salinger's daughter. It felt both surreal and very real.

I loved it.

I don't remember how long we stayed at the bar, but I'll never forget being back at the Kennedy house and David walking into Suzanne's and my bedroom right after we'd changed into nightgowns. He (nicely) grabbed my arms and led me to the hallway surrounding all the bedrooms on the second floor. Some pretty heavy kissing thus ensued. (We were kissing outside the bedrooms of the sleeping Ethel Kennedy and Roger Mudd and his wife. *Say what?)*

In 1978, I was finally facing my sexuality, but that was not the reason I declined more romance with David that night. I had a feeling, just a little inkling, something might go a little awry, and I didn't want anything negative to happen. I didn't want to cause any type of distress to Mrs. Kennedy or Suzanne. And I'm not saying anything negative about David here either. He was very kind and appealing. And he made it easy for me to say thank you for a very nice evening—and good night.

I saw him one last time, the next day, as Suzanne and I were driving out of the driveway for Logan Airport and Washington. David leaned into the car and said

CHAPTER 10: DREAMS COME TRUE

goodbye with very direct, warm eye contact and a smile.

Despite valiant reported efforts at drug treatment, David would die of a drug overdose nearly six years later. So very sad. I'll certainly never forget him. He added a special glow to my dream weekend.

I slept like a baby after we got back from the bar and David and I had had our "moment."

After showering the next morning, Suzanne and I were told to simply tell the kitchen what we'd like for breakfast. We can have anything? Sure, just tell them. Sounded good to us! I think I asked for French Toast, orange juice, and coffee. I recall a newspaper of some sort being passed around while we drank coffee with Roger Mudd and exchanging light conversation with him and Mrs. Mudd.

A group of us then continued to drink coffee on the front porch. All of a sudden, Ethel appeared and asked if we'd like to go sailing. **Ah, Yeah**. She told me to follow her as she drove her convertible through Hyannis Port until we got to their sailboat in Hyannis. So, get this:

Suzanne, Gregory, and I were again in my rental. **I was asked *by* Ethel Kennedy to follow directly**

behind her(!) Her convertible top was down as she drove. Tourists recognized her and cried out in excitement. They also waved and smiled at *me*, at my car!

I was no longer a tourist hungering for a look at a Kennedy. Now, I was part of the *Kennedy entourage*, getting ready to **sail** with them. *Ah, life can be so good.*

We got to the sailboat with ease. I parked and Suzanne, her brother, and I got on board. "What did you say your name is?" Mrs. Kennedy asked me. "Jenny."

"Well, Jenny, when you sail with the Kennedys, you have to help out." **Gulp**. Was this a foreboding of something scary, like Touch Football on the Sea? But I jauntily replied, "Of course. How can I help?"

"You're sitting on the cooler holding sandwiches for lunch. The type of sandwich is marked on each one. When it's time, can you pass them out?"

"Sure. Happy to." (***Relief!***)

Suzanne and I loved our afternoon sailing. Everyone was relaxed and happy. Young Douglas (around 11) was singing and then suddenly stopped. I remember

CHAPTER 10: DREAMS COME TRUE

smiling when Ethel said how much she enjoyed hearing him sing and to please continue (which he did). It was a clear, beautiful day. All of a sudden, Mrs. Kennedy exclaimed, "Is that Eunice over there?" It was. We sailed closer to her boat and someone suggested we race against each other. Game on!

It didn't take long to see the Kennedy competitive spirit in action. I just sat back and marveled at it all: I'm sailing on Nantucket Sound with the Kennedys, on Robert and Ethel Kennedy's sailboat. I'm on Ethel's team, competing against Eunice Kennedy Shriver. Eunice is the founder of the Special Olympics, the sister of Jack, Bobby, and Ted Kennedy, and the mother of Maria Shriver, who has a burgeoning career in broadcasting in 1978. We won the race. ***Don't you just love Sundays like this?***

Suzanne's and my flight back to Washington was scheduled for later that evening, so we expressed our thanks to Mrs. Kennedy and said our goodbyes after the sail. What an incredible, action-packed two days. I found Gregory Salinger so darling and delightful. I googled his name recently. He's a very handsome fifty-something executive with Apax Partners and seems to have spent much of his life in both France and the U.S.

The next day, back at work in Senator Muskie's office, you can imagine the swarm of interested co-workers. I was on Cloud Nine for days.

To show how times have changed, young people these days have little or no experience with the drama and trauma of "long distance" telephone calls we older folks remember all too well. No cell phones in the 1970s, big expenses to call out-of-state, much less out-of-country. My parents were visiting France from the time Suzanne asked me to accompany her to Hyannis Port until sometime after my return. I never gave a thought to calling my parents in Paris with the news: too expensive. Kind of hard to believe now. However, my grandparents, aunts, uncles, cousins, and friends galore certainly heard from me, along with my siblings. Their vicarious thrill was palpable. Later, when Mom and Dad reached California at the end of their trip, they immediately called Mom's parents in Maine to say they were home safely. My grandmother exclaimed, "Have you heard Jenny's news that she and Pierre Salinger's daughter spent the weekend at the Kennedy Compound as guests of Ethel Kennedy? They spent the night there and went sailing with Ethel and several of her children?" Mom said her initial reaction to this flabbergasting news was, "Oh, No! Mummy has developed dementia!"

CHAPTER 10: DREAMS COME TRUE

I shudder when I think I almost blew going on this excursion with Suzanne, an excursion that energized me and thrilled me for the rest of my life. How wonderful, too, that 46 years after those spectacular days, Ethel Kennedy is still going strong at age 96. She and Suzanne gave me the best weekend I could ever imagine.

Adequate expressions of gratitude escape me.

CHAPTER 11

THE WHITE HOUSE STAFF 1979-1981

CHAPTER 11: THE WHITE HOUSE STAFF

I was on a roll, it surely seemed, after my Hyannis Port extravaganza in August of 1978. So why not pursue a job on the White House Staff in 1979? Someone said she'd heard there was an opening on Vice President Walter F. Mondale's staff (President Jimmy Carter's VP) — at about the same time I was silently reaching the end of my rope working with a very difficult woman on Senator Muskie's staff. Many other staff members were aware of her temperament that never seemed to improve. She was very bright and hardworking, but I (and others) surmised she was never going to leave. So I thought, after 4½ years, it was time for me to move on.

A further inspiration came one day as I walked to the Russell Senate Office Building from my apartment. I was on my usual route going by the U.S. Supreme Court when the guy who regularly mowed the lawn there suddenly shut off the motor and walked over to me. "Can I ask you a question?"

"Sure," I replied cheerfully.

"Why is it you always look so angry?"

Splat. I wasn't expecting that! I thought I faked or suppressed my intimidation and anger at my co-worker better than that. I told this nice man I worked with a difficult woman and had to steel myself each day against her onslaught of criticisms of me and other co-workers. I thanked him (sincerely). A lesson learned. Yes — time to move on.

I was also intrigued to interview for the job because interviews were being held in the enormous Old Executive Office Building (now named the Eisenhower Executive Office Building) with its dramatic French Second Empire architecture. The "EOB" (or "OEOB") was located right next to the White House. The building was once known as the largest office building in the world and had held the Departments of State, War, and Navy in the past. In more recent times, it had become the office building for staff members of both the president and vice president of the United States, among others. Walter Mondale was the first vice president to have an office not only in the EOB but also at the White House. A couple of Vice President Mondale's staffers also had their offices in the White House. Space was very limited there, but the prestige of having your desk inside the White House versus the EOB (where offices typically had tall ceilings and pleasing amounts of space) led to reduced office expectations and demands. One top Mondale aide literally had his desk placed inside a regular closet, with the closet door I believe removed. *But he could boast of having an office in the White House.* The office for my prospective

CHAPTER 11: THE WHITE HOUSE STAFF

job would be in the Old Executive Office Building—just fine with me!

D.C. had an impressive new subway system with an easy connection from my apartment on Capitol Hill to the White House. I decided the job move was meant to be—so I pursued it with gusto, but also the freedom that comes when you know you have nothing to lose. I still had the Muskie job and realized my being hired for the White House Staff as a 27-year-old female in late 1978 or 1979 might be a long shot.

I asked Madeleine Albright, my former Muskie colleague, if she would serve as a reference for me. (Yes, *that* Madeleine Albright. Madeleine became the first female U.S. Secretary of State when President Bill Clinton appointed her in 1997, which was then the highest political office achieved by any woman in U.S. history.) Madeleine had left Senator Muskie's staff the year before to join the White House Staff of President Jimmy Carter. She had been Senator Muskie's chief Legislative Assistant, and I was one of his two Legislative Correspondents (we composed his responses to constituent and national mail). Madeleine's desk was very near mine. We laughed easily with each other, had interesting conversations, and shared our personal vulnerabilities. I felt we had a good connection and was pleased when she said she'd be delighted to serve as a reference. (A footnote to my reference list: this was late 1978, before Madeleine had become a national and international figure requiring confidentiality. Her home address and home phone number were clearly listed.)

I have no idea if Madeleine was ever contacted as a reference, but I do know I got the job as Advance Coordinator for Vice President Walter F. Mondale! I interviewed with several Mondale staffers in that intimidating but grand building with its black-and-white checkered hall flooring — and I made it! I began work in February of 1979 in a good-sized office, just a matter of yards from the vice president's, on the second floor. A driveway separated our building from the White House. I would soon wear a White House Staff identity necklace around my neck. Both the EOB and White House were secured buildings, and I had to pass an FBI security clearance process. This process was more "interesting" than I'd imagined. One of my sisters said her somewhat snooty neighbor on one side of her house treated her and her family with noticeably greater respect after the FBI had actually interviewed *her* (the neighbor) as a check on the kind of people *my sister and her family represented.* In contrast, the neighbor on the other side, upon hearing the FBI was knocking on his door, raced to flush items down his toilet. *Such a loss! What is going on???*

CHAPTER 11: THE WHITE HOUSE STAFF

Many Americans wonder what a vice president of the United States actually does. The limited responsibilities of many previous occupants of that office and the limited communications between many presidents and their vice presidents were a source of concern that inspired both Walter Mondale, who was an active and highly respected U.S. senator, and Jimmy Carter to make significant changes. Thus, Walter Mondale was the first vice president to have an office inside the White House (as well as the EOB) and the Mondale staff was more integrated into the rest of the White House staff. We were truly part of the same team. President Carter expanded Vice President Mondale's role and responsibilities and regularly conferred with him. Walter Mondale served as a full partner of President Carter.

Vice presidents travel, both domestically and overseas. They can be the president's eyes and ears as they meet with constituents throughout the U.S. and stay apprised of national issues and concerns. The same is true for foreign affairs, as well as the need to attend funerals and important events in other countries. A team of "Advance" people typically precedes the arrival of the vice president to a particular local event or events in various states or countries. They work with local dignitaries or their designees to plan events, establish timelines, and organize other logistics to meet desired outcomes or to enhance the look and feel of an event (such as selecting a smaller venue for an event when a less than optimal turnout appears likely).

MY RESPONSIBILITIES ON THE WHITE HOUSE STAFF

I served as Vice President Mondale's Senior Advance Coordinator. My job was to handle logistics for his domestic and foreign travels. "Senior" was added to my title a few months after I began when I was able to demonstrate the huge turnover in my job—I believe five people in two years—was at least in part due to the need for two people to handle all the fast-moving parts. A second coordinator was soon added and that made a huge difference. (Thanks, dear friend, Patti Stoll.)

I was responsible for getting the advance men and women on the road or in the air and back, coordinate with the Secret Service and White House Communications Agency (WHCA) staff on hotel arrangements, and order extra vehicles for the vice-presidential motorcades. When travel involved official business, I used the White House Travel Office for airline requirements. I then directly called various hotels or motels throughout the U.S., trying to book only unionized facilities, if possible. This was especially

CHAPTER 11: THE WHITE HOUSE STAFF

important if Vice President Mondale would be spending the night.

For campaign events, I worked with campaign staff to make sure they made appropriate and accurate travel arrangements, as well as paid for them. (When the vice president travels on *official* business, the U.S. government picks up the tab. However, if the vice president is participating in *political* activities, the Democratic Party or the campaign is responsible.) These legal distinctions were important, but also made my job more difficult. I was still very much involved in his political travels because Walter Mondale did not cease to be vice president of the United States when he was campaigning. *Official* staff was still necessary. But to keep *political* expenses and activities separate and legal, I had to coordinate with political or campaign staff.

I vividly remember one "glitch" along these lines. A U.S. senator and his wife were traveling on behalf of the Carter/Mondale campaign in 1980. As I recall, they were traveling from their home in Washington, D.C. to some campaign event in another state. I told the campaign staff to take care of the airplane tickets and other logistical needs of this senator and his wife. A campaign staffer then called me with the travel details. When he told me their flight involved a 7AM departure from Dulles Airport the next day, I questioned the 7AM versus PM time and he assured me this was correct and the best arrangement available. I gave the information to the couple. And you can imagine how much I loved hearing from them—after they'd driven all the way out to Dulles Airport in Virginia in the wee hours of the morning—only to discover their flight was indeed for that *night – 7PM, not 7AM.*

The senator and his wife were actually very gracious about the faux pas (at least to me). This snafu brings to mind another *delicious* story. I told the Dulles air flight story to my friend Dolores Stover a few years after it happened. She laughed uproariously when I disclosed the names of the senator and his wife. After serving as Senator Muskie's (and Ted Kennedy's) personal secretary, Dolores had worked as an executive assistant at the elegant Georgetown home of the honorable Averell Harriman and his wife, Pamela Churchill Harriman (former daughter-in-law of Winston Churchill). Dolores had either observed or was told about a *major* faux pas by this *very same* senator during a dinner party at the Harriman house years before. King Hussein of Jordan and his new American wife, Queen Noor, were in Washington, D.C. in 1980 being feted by President and Mrs. Carter. Queen Noor was the former Lisa Halaby of Washington, D.C. and the daughter of Najeeb Halaby, chairman of Pan American World Airways.

CHAPTER 11: THE WHITE HOUSE STAFF

Not long after King Hussein and Queen Noor returned to Jordan, the Harrimans threw a dinner party at their Georgetown home. Their guest list included Mr. and Mrs. Najeeb Halaby (Queen Noor's parents) and also *this very senator and his wife*. Well, as things got started, the senator began chatting with Mrs. Halaby, apparently not realizing her identity. When she made a reference to her daughter and an airline, the senator cheerfully asked, "Is your daughter a stewardess?" Her pointed reply: "My daughter is the Queen."

I felt so much better about the 7AM airport mistake.

My Advance Coordinator job could be exciting and exhausting. There was a four-day period during the 1980 campaign when I was in charge of travel logistics involving 80 advance people in 25 cities simultaneously. It, of course, required the usual legal separations between official and campaign business and made my *make-sure-it-all-gets-done* official responsibilities more complicated.

Advance men and women come from a variety of backgrounds and professions, some living in the Washington, D.C. area but most live throughout the U.S. They usually have experience in event planning and related logistical details. They sometimes performed advance work full-time for us (and other political leaders) or they worked in professions that allowed periodic separations to perform advance work. My boss, Director of Advance Dick Schmitt, selected and guided the advance teams as they performed their myriad tasks.

Here's a little something that can mess up smooth operations. A small change in plans, especially at the last minute, can have a serious unraveling effect.

Vice President Mondale (or the political staff) decided to make a last-minute change to my 80-advance-people-in-25-cities-simultaneously scenario. Most of the advance teams involved individuals flying in from different cities or states—either from their individual homes and jobs or from different just-completed advance trips. An "advance team" consists of several people working together on *a particular trip or event*. (It's not the same people working together most of the time.)

Let's say advance man Ed just completed a Mondale trip to New York/Manhattan and now needs to fly to an upcoming Mondale event in Des Moines, Iowa. Let's say advance woman Kate has completed a Minneapolis advance and now plans to join Ed—so Kate requires a flight from Minnesota to Des Moines. Finally, advance man Chuck has gotten time off from his job in Boston and requires a flight to Des Moines so he can help Ed and Kate. Let's say Ed is selected

CHAPTER 11: THE WHITE HOUSE STAFF

for the advance team in Chicago immediately following the Des Moines event, while Kate is not scheduled for Chicago but to lead a team after Des Moines and Chicago for a Mondale trip to Iowa City. Let's say Chuck has to return to his Boston job immediately after Des Moines, so his personal schedule is tight. **Now imagine:** airline tickets to Des Moines have been bought by the campaign for Ed, Kate, and Chuck at their individual locations. I have informed them about their flights, plus the location of their Des Moines hotel. I've notified the Secret Service and White House Communications Agency staff of these details so they can make their own arrangements. I've ordered Des Moines motorcade cars. Dick Schmitt is filling the team in on Des Moines event details. **(Please remember there are also 24 other cities, each with its own advance team actively preparing, in these back-to-back Mondale trips.)**

Imagine my getting a call at home around **midnight** during this drama, a call saying a change needed to be made ASAP to the vice president's upcoming Iowa trip. **There won't be a Des Moines stop** right now. Later, yes. Soon, yes. But not right now. Ed, Kate, and Chuck were already in the air to Des Moines from their three different locations. **This is 1980. No cell phones, no email, no other social media communication systems**.

Panic. What city in what state is replacing Des Moines? Same event timelines? Ed, Kate, and Chuck still the right team? Any new hotel ideas? Hurry—cancel flights, hotels, motorcade cars; inform the Secret Service and Communications folks ASAP. Immediately make new flight arrangements to the new city. Somehow alert Ed, Kate, and Chuck about the switch *while they're flying* on three different airplanes to Des Moines.

Are you catching my drift? A little ol' travel change or two can unravel many moving parts. (Then, have fun delegating work and payments to the campaign staff to keep things legal. In the middle of the night.)

I don't remember the exact city or cities that were involved in the above changes or many of the details about *how* everything resolved, but I do remember everything, finally, got reconfigured. I vaguely remember learning how to communicate with Ed, Kate, and Chuck on board their planes and redirecting them. The scramble exhausted me for days. Many adrenalin laughs and a martini **or two** surely helped.

FLYING ON AIR FORCE II

Thinking about vice presidential travels brings the subject of Air Force II to mind. The designation of

CHAPTER 11: THE WHITE HOUSE STAFF

"Air Force II" is made when the vice president of the United States is on board one of these special airplanes, while "Air Force I" indicates the president. My Advance Office position was a "desk job," but I was asked to travel with Vice President Mondale five times during my two years on his staff. These were domestic trips, but I heard I would join him for his very next overseas excursion—had we won the 1980 election instead of Ronald Reagan and George H. W. Bush. (Another reason to regret our loss!) My being asked to accompany the vice president had less to do with work responsibilities on the road (at least for me) than a chance for me to acquire direct knowledge about vice presidential trips and the responsibilities of advance teams in action. I also felt it was a thank you from my superiors for an often-frantic desk job being well done. (Or I like to think so!) I'll certainly never forget my first ride on Air Force II—and *not* for reasons you might expect.

A big, shiny black, White House car took traveling staffers from the Executive Office Building out to Andrews Air Force Base in Maryland. I thought, *Such a smooth and nice way to get to the airport.* We were headed to an official event in Ohio. The staff seating arrangement on Air Force II was certainly way more spacious and comfortable than a commercial airplane set-up. The words to the popular Virginia Slims cigarette advertisement popped into my head as I took off with the vice president of the United States: *You've Come A Long Way, Baby!*

Well, not too long after takeoff, *Long Way Baby* noticed a concerned look on the faces of the Secret Service Agents sitting nearby. **Is something wrong?** I quietly asked. No answer. Then came an announcement saying we would be making an emergency landing. My maiden voyage on Air Force II and we're making **An Emergency Landing**! So many times in my life, gloriously lucky things happened, and I'd think, *What were the odds of this wonderful thing happening?* Now I'm thinking, *Is Air Force II going to crash? Is someone trying to attack the vice president? The president? What are the odds I'd be on Air Force II — **for the first time — when it had to make its very first ever Emergency Landing?*** Controlled anxiety took hold of all of us.

Word was (I think I recall this correctly), a light that should have come on to indicate something important, didn't come on. Wouldn't come on. That either meant there was simply a light-related issue **or** there was a serious mechanical problem. We were told we needed to get on the ground ASAP. We steeled ourselves for the emergency landing process. One of my co-workers whispered to me, "I heard the Secret Service marching orders are: **Get him off the plane!**"

CHAPTER 11: THE WHITE HOUSE STAFF

"Who's Him?" I stupidly asked.

"The Vice President."

"Oh, yes, of course, of course." OMG, *What's happening?*

I can't remember where we landed or how long we stayed there. But I do remember the ultimate answer: just a light issue. Phew!

Long Way Baby gratefully slept that night.

OTHER WHITE HOUSE STAFF "BENEFITS"

The joy of everything else returned that morning when I got to participate in my very first Vice Presidential motorcade through the town. An adrenalin rush, for sure. I sat in one of several cars lined up behind Vice President Mondale's shiny car, its little flags blowing in the wind. Numerous policemen were on motorcycles beside and ahead of us, their headlights shining while they revved their engines. Then, suddenly, the policemen took off and so, of course, did the Vice President of the United States and the rest of the motorcade procession. The motorcycles helped guide and protect us as we moved through the town. Town folks lined up excitedly smiling, waving, and taking pictures. Parents were happily explaining what was happening to their cheering youngsters. Then, when we arrived at our destination, citizens rushed towards us as we exited our vehicles. They wanted autographs—yes, even from staffers such as me. *Long Way Baby* was very, very, very happy.

Another exciting White House Staff perk or "responsibility" that I hadn't anticipated involved sometimes being asked to stand on the South Lawn of the White House when foreign leaders were in town meeting with the President and Vice President. Think of all the national news coverage when a world leader comes to Washington and how many times we citizens watch news footage of speeches by those leaders and ours, as well as their signing ceremonies for important documents. Did you ever wonder who comprises the "audience" on the White House grounds? It often consists of a variety of important people—Cabinet members, senators, members of Congress, as well as other American leaders and those from the foreign country being honored. But it sometimes also consists of White House staff members. Their attendance may stem from relevant work they've performed, or they might be asked to attend in an effort to increase the size of the audience. We want important visitors to feel our warm welcome.

CHAPTER 11: THE WHITE HOUSE STAFF

You'll recall my previous discussion of King Hussein of Jordan and his new American wife, Queen Noor. I was asked to temporarily drop everything I was busily working on one day in 1980 and head to the South Lawn of the White House. I didn't initially understand why and was rather irritated. *I don't have time to go stand on the damn lawn.* It didn't take me long, however, to come to my senses. I soon learned the President of the United States wanted the White House Staff to stand on the South Lawn and join an impressive group observing history in the making by President Carter—the Leader of the Free World—and our ally, King Hussein of Jordan. **Why, I do think I can squeeze this in after all!**

Here's another example of special White House moments.

In April of 1980, President Carter ordered the U.S. Armed Forces to attempt to rescue 52 embassy staff members who were being held captive at the U.S. Embassy in Tehran, Iran. The rescue attempt failed disastrously and played a significant role in the Carter-Mondale election loss later that year.

In an effort to show our sympathy and support for President Jimmy Carter, the entire White House Staff was called to a meeting in the elegant East Room.

Beautiful chandeliers adorned the ceiling of the room, which has graced so many historic events. We sat on golden-colored chairs. At least one of President Carter's sisters was there. I recall Vice President Mondale, among others, speaking eloquently about standing by President Carter at this devastating time. I'm not sure how long we gathered, but every minute seemed important. I think all of us in attendance were very moved. Our East Room meeting helped us all pull together at a very emotional time.

Many years later, when I was no longer living in Washington, I worked at a good, but much less wondrous, job. We were called to a staff meeting in a messy little room. Boxes were stacked everywhere. Things were in disarray because construction improvements were in the works. One of my co-workers, who knew about my White House days, looked at me with a smile and said, "This must make you feel like you're back in the White House." "I was just thinking the same thing," I smiled back. I looked around the unkempt, tiny room. "All we need is a couple of chandeliers and I'd swear I was sitting in the East Room!"

Ah, all the different days and ways of our lives.

CHAPTER 11: THE WHITE HOUSE STAFF

AFTER THE WHITE HOUSE DAYS

America's democracy is typically on profound display when the current office holder—the current leader—loses the next election and thus must step down and let the newly elected leader take over. The transition to new leaders had gone quite smoothly over all the years of the USA—until Donald J. Trump changed all that in 2021. Most of us never realized how lucky we had been.

The Carter-Mondale election loss in November 1980 was anticipated, but maybe not in so crushing a way as in only winning a handful of states. Rampaging inflation, serious problems in Iran, and the growing popularity of Ronald Reagan presented President Carter with seemingly insurmountable election challenges. I'm glad Jimmy Carter and Walter Mondale lived long enough to see some of the administration's reputation restored or at least meriting a more nuanced critique.

A President and Vice President's personal staff members typically also lose their jobs after an election loss. That now included 29-year-old me. We wound things down during the transition following Election Day in early November 1980 and the swearing-in of the new leaders on January 20, 1981. During the transition period, one of my co-workers suggested I look up from my desk in the Old Executive Office Building. My door was open. "Watch this! This is historic," he said. Outgoing Vice President Walter F. Mondale and soon-to-be Vice President George H. W. Bush were walking down the hallway. The old guard was showing the new one around. Yes, a moment in history, a fine display of democracy. But sad if you hoped to win and concerning if your political beliefs significantly differed. I felt both emotions.

On our final day, I was given the choice of turning in my White House Staff badge or having it punched as expired. I have kept it all these years with its little expired holes. Here's something jolting: once the last day arrives and the badges are turned in or "fixed," a staffer from the outgoing administration who realizes he or she has left a personal item behind in the EOB must get official approval to re-enter the building. Talk about **Being In** and **Now You Are Out**. It's kind of rattling—and also wonderful: democracy in action.

I needed a new job and Washington seemed to swarm with Republicans...so I decided to become a real estate agent! The brother of one of my Mondale pals used to come into our office raving about all the money he was making as a realtor. *"Get your license, Jenny. You'd be great at it and make so much more money!"*

CHAPTER 11: THE WHITE HOUSE STAFF

I started a multiple-week real estate course in Virginia right after we left office and then passed the realtor exam. I became a licensed agent at the newly opened Capitol Hill Office of Shannon & Luchs, on upper Pennsylvania Avenue. Once again, I could easily walk to work, but this time in the opposite direction of the Capitol Building. How'd I do? Pretty darn well, especially since interest rates were breathtakingly high and constantly growing. Listing and selling houses wasn't really my thing, though, so nearly two years later, in late 1982, I made another change. A really big one. I decided to say goodbye to being a realtor and goodbye to my beloved Washington, D.C. and my many friends there. I decided to return to my home state of California after eight years. I had largely made my Washington, D.C. dreams come true and felt a good sense of accomplishment. The Republican takeover reduced my interest in pursuing another political job at that time. I was 31. My health problems remained, but at a less intense level most of the time.

I had solidly "come out of the closet" in my own mind and told a few (straight) friends and my siblings. I was not yet ready to tell my parents. I'd been pouring myself into the exciting yet exhausting Mondale job and then working hard to learn and excel at my new realtor career. My dating life was mostly non-existent. Since I'd largely settled on my health issues being caused by my homophobic fears, I increasingly worried I'd reverse my progress if I didn't seriously work on those issues. California seemed a much easier place to accomplish that and, I hoped, to eventually find a female partner. The thought of being near my parents and siblings, as well as friends in Arcata and San Francisco, also made me happy.

At the end of August 1982, my plane from Washington, D.C. touched down in San Francisco. The sky was a glistening blue. I had mixed emotions about what was ahead, but decided the gorgeous sky was leading the way.

I made the right decision.

CHAPTER 12

BACK TO CALIFORNIA

1982 *and* ONWARD

BETTY AT LAST

CHAPTER 12: BACK TO CALIFORNIA

My re-emergence into California went well. I stayed with my cousin Johnna Wood at her apartment on Polk Street in San Francisco while I found an apartment of my own and got a job. With Johnna's help, I lucked out again by finding a fabulous one-bedroom apartment on Nob Hill, just down from Grace Cathedral and the Fairmont Hotel for only $400 a month. And it was rent-controlled. That meant I could make a modest salary and still afford to live there by myself. I wanted to find a fun, relatively easy job. No more work excuses for why I wasn't pursuing romance! I found such a job at a San Francisco radio station, GE/NBC-owned KNBR. I worked there from January 1983 until late summer 1989. It did the trick in every category.

I was a "sales coordinator" in the very active KNBR Sales Department. My position was largely administrative until we added some bells and whistles later on. I hired additional coordinators and served as their supervisor but was careful to keep things on the "fun and easy" level. My bosses and co-workers were great people, and we surely knew how to laugh and party together! We genuinely enjoyed being in each other's company. Several of my KNBR co-workers remain special friends.

In early 1987, I met Betty Hirschfeld through mutual friends, and love blossomed so beautifully. We happily dated for almost a year before I moved into her house a few miles north of the Golden Gate Bridge, in Mill Valley. We celebrated 37 years together in early 2024! We both feel very fortunate.

My "eclectic" (which I like) career path continued. Now that I lived in Marin County, California and had a wonderful, settled personal life, I decided to join a behavioral health (mental health) company in nearby Larkspur in 1990. I ultimately became the Director of Account Management for the company. The management position and large rise in pay nurtured my ego, but the toxic atmosphere with company acquisitions and seemingly endless changes in management finally got to me. I said goodbye at the beginning of 1999, after nearly ten years.

Difficult as some of those years could be, I still embrace memories from that account management job. My favorite occurred before I became the department director. This involved securing the contract for the Lucasfilm "EAP" — the Employee Assistance Program for employees of the George Lucas/*Star Wars* company. Our Vice President of Sales drove us out to George Lucas's famous Skywalker Ranch one day in nearby San Rafael. As we neared the extraordinary property, she calmly said, "Jenny, my understanding is that securing the contract has come down to our company or [our main

CHAPTER 12: BACK TO CALIFORNIA

competitor]. The focus now is their comfort level with each company's designated account manager. I don't mean to freak you out, Jenny, but you're it, so it's up to you today." She then offered me a very bright smile!

Fortunately, the Lucasfilm staff made the process very comfortable. They were easy to talk to, asked good questions, and came across as sharp, likeable people. *And, thankfully, we got the contract!*

I soon started performing trainings on the EAP services my company offered, such as mental health counseling, eldercare assistance, and legal guidance. These trainings took place for all Lucas employees who worked in the many buildings at Skywalker Ranch, as well as other nearby company locations. It was quite a daunting experience. (I loved it.) It was fun to see the original Yoda and other original Lucasfilm paraphernalia at the ranch. I mean, how often does a trainer finish her day with a walk by George Lucas's very own Yoda—who's smiling at her? (Or was I smiling at Yoda as I passed by?) Hey-*we were smiling at each other!*

I was 47 and wondered what I now wanted in a career. I knew I no longer wanted a management role. I preferred having my own "ballgame"—focusing on and performing tasks that were my responsibility and not having to be responsible for a staff. But, for the first time ever, I had absolutely no idea what I sought. I was starting to get nervous about this unfamiliar feeling until one Sunday, Betty said, "The *San Francisco Chronicle* shows Jenny Craig is looking for weight loss counselors." As a former Jenny Craig client, I did a double take. A few people over the years had told me I should be a psychologist, but I never seriously entertained the idea. I knew this could be a mini-version of that. I believed in the Jenny Craig weight loss program and I liked the food. I enjoyed people. I exclaimed to Betty, "This could be great! I'll do it for the next year or two. It'll be my 'bridge job' while I figure out what I really want to do next. This is perfect!"

I was soon hired as a "consultant" (weight loss counselor) at Jenny Craig's location in Marin County. *And I liked the job*. I stayed in the position for 18 years until I retired in 2017 at age 66.

I found being a consultant at Jenny Craig very fulfilling. I worked with so many interesting clients. Some were very prominent citizens, even famous, while others seemed to represent those from backgrounds of poverty, alcoholism/drug abuse, and related challenges. There were intriguing characters with dramatic life stories, as well as many whom I simply enjoyed knowing. Several clients told me secrets they said they'd never told anyone else, not even their therapist. I was so moved by this. In fact, I was so moved that I decided to write a book entitled, *What Did Uncle Harold Know?*, which was published in 2016. Those Jenny Craig clients who so honored me with their stories got me wondering what kind of secrets or vulnerable disclosures my great-uncle, Harold Mitchell, might have heard during his long bartending career at New York's famous Copacabana and the great Sands Hotel in Las Vegas. Uncle Harold had died by then, so I sought insights and answers by interviewing a variety of other bartenders. Talk about interesting....

My Jenny Craig responsibilities contained just enough of a counseling role to satisfy my interest in people and desire to help, while also providing the added attraction that comes from being able to actually *see* the results of what you do for a living. Joy can come from all sorts of weight loss goals and results. But, wow, try working with a woman who was initially in tears over her weight and her difficulties losing it. You say, "If you hold on to me, I promise I'll hold on to you." She says, Yes. What a ride unfolded for both of us over the next couple of years. Initial weight in the mid-300s...then down, down, down to the mid-200s. Then down, down, down to 150. She felt so much better, was so much healthier, and looked so happy in her new wardrobe.

Now, years later, I'm told this client periodically returns to use the Jenny Craig services when her weight creeps back up. That's just what I wanted to hear. (Many weight issues tend to be chronic for a variety of reasons. A wise motto: Find a healthy "fix" that works for you. Employ the fix, ideally, before things get way out of hand. Consider this as having a "tune-up." If things "get way out of hand" — which can happen to the best of us — a good weight loss service should be nothing but a support and help for you. Don't be embarrassed to return!)

Phew. What a variety of jobs I have had!

I think variety is good. It stretches knowledge and skills and offers different types of appreciation. I think I might have achieved a much bigger career had I not gotten Multiple Sclerosis and encountered such a convoluted diagnostic process. I regularly watch the women who have political shows on MSNBC TV and elsewhere. They can make me feel wistful for what I sometimes dream might have been. Maybe I'm an arrogant fool, but I believe I have at least some of their talents. All the years of the awful MS symptoms and the diagnosis mess cut into my strength and energy. The doctors really did a number on my mind, too. I tried not to let that happen, but good luck with that. They were the "experts." All of it took a huge toll. I am angry at those early doctors. Mostly, though, I'm extra glad I accomplished what I did.

And wasn't it grand? Did I convey how grand? I mean, I *promised* myself going down the hill to my grammar school at age 12, the day after President Kennedy was assassinated, that I would—**yes, I would**—bring the Kennedys and other important people into my life. I didn't tell anyone because, *how ridiculous is that?*

Then: Suzanne and Pierre Salinger. A Capitol Hill job with Senator Edmund S. Muskie. A job on The White House Staff for Vice President Walter F. Mondale. The weekend at the Kennedy Compound. Sailing with Ethel Kennedy and so many members of her family. David Kennedy. Madeleine Albright. Barbara Gamarekian. Chris Matthews. Oh, and a man named Joe Biden! I was his intern as he began his U.S. Senate career in 1973. The same Joe Biden who became President of the United States in 2021.

The President of the United States.

Beyond even my wildest dreams.

I'm so happy. Thanks, Everyone.

CHAPTER 13

LETTERS & PHOTOS
From the Author's Personal Collection

**SOMETIMES
DREAMS DO
COME TRUE**

PHOTO OF SUZANNE SALINGER (L)
AND THE AUTHOR, JENNY WOOD.
CAPE COD, MASSACHUSETTS, AUGUST 1978.

THIS BLURRY PHOTO IS THE ONLY KNOWN
PHOTO OF THE TWO OF THEM.

UNKNOWN PHOTOGRAPHER, CENTERVILLE,
MASSACHUSETTS, 1978

BARBARA GAMAREKIAN AT HER GEORGETOWN HOME WITH THE AUTHOR, OCTOBER 2003

PHOTOGRAPHER: BETTY HIRSCHFELD, WASHINGTON, D.C., 2003

BARBARA WAS AN ASSISTANT IN THE WHITE HOUSE PRESS OFFICE OF PRESIDENT JOHN F. KENNEDY. THE PRESS OFFICE WAS HEADED BY PRESS SECRETARY PIERRE SALINGER.

CHAPTER 13: LETTERS AND PHOTOS

EVEN THOUGH THE AUTHOR AND BARBARA GAMAREKIAN DIDN'T EVEN KNOW JEHANNE BIETRY SALINGER-CARLSON (PIERRE SALINGER'S MOTHER), JEHANNE WROTE A LETTER OF INTRODUCTION FOR THE TWO WOMEN.

A WONDERFUL FRIENDSHIP WAS BORN.

BARBARA GAMAREKIAN DIED OF CANCER FOUR MONTHS AFTER THIS PICTURE WAS TAKEN.

Defying Adversity as I Race to Achieve My Dreams

NO PICTURE WAS TAKEN OF THE AUTHOR WITH SENATOR JOSEPH R. BIDEN, JR. HOWEVER, PLEASE SEE THE HANDWRITTEN THANK YOU LETTER HE WROTE TO HER ON 6-20-1973.

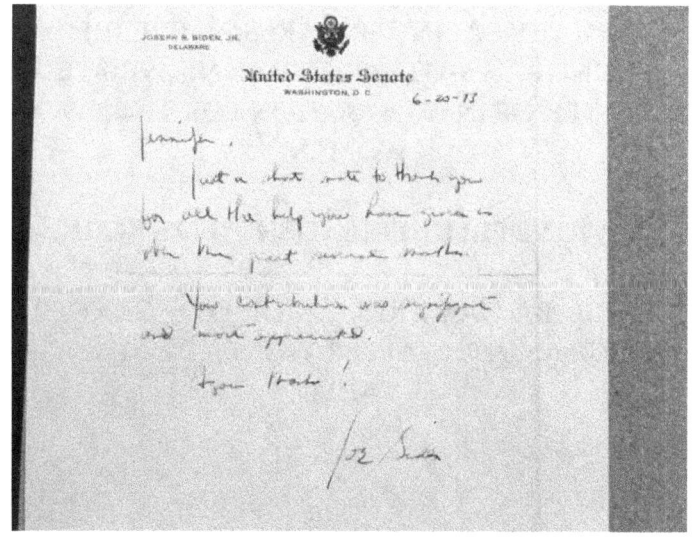

IT SAYS:

Jennifer, Just a short note to thank you for all the help you have given us over the past several months. Your contribution was significant and most appreciated. Again, thanks! Joe Biden.

THE AUTHOR WITH SENATOR EDMUND S. MUSKIE IN HIS OFFICE AT THE RUSSELL SENATE OFFICE BUILDING ON CAPITOL HILL. HE WROTE ON 2-28-1979:

To Jenny Wood. My thanks and warm good wishes,
Ed Muskie

UNKNOWN PHOTOGRAPHER, U.S. SENATE, WASHINGTON, D.C., 1979

Defying Adversity as I Race to Achieve My Dreams

THE AUTHOR WITH VICE PRESIDENT WALTER F. MONDALE AT THE VICE-PRESIDENTIAL HOME IN WASHINGTON, D.C., 1979.

UNKNOWN PHOTOGRAPHER, NAVAL OBSERVATORY, WASHINGTON, D.C., 1979

CHAPTER 13: LETTERS AND PHOTOS

THE AUTHOR WITH PRESIDENT JIMMY CARTER IN THE WHITE HOUSE OVAL OFFICE, 1980

UNKNOWN PHOTOGRAPHER, THE WHITE HOUSE, WASHINGTON, D.C., 1980

Defying Adversity as I Race to Achieve My Dreams

A PERSONAL LETTER TO THE AUTHOR FROM HER FORMER MUSKIE COLLEAGUE, SECRETARY OF STATE MADELEINE ALBRIGHT, 1999

THE SECRETARY OF STATE
WASHINGTON

March 18, 1999

Dear Jenny:

I recently received your lovely letter. It was so good to hear from you.

This job is amazing and I love it. There are days, of course, when I just want to run away - at least for a few minutes. There are also many rewarding and historic times. Sometimes I still need to pinch myself to believe this is real.

Your positive critique means a lot to me. When the demands are overwhelming, knowing I have people like you in my corner helps to reenergize me.

With warm regards,

Sincerely,

Madeleine

Madeleine K. Albright

Ms. Jenny Wood,
    37 Bayview Terrace,
        Mill Valley, California 94941.

CHAPTER 14

GOODBYE, SUZANNE SALINGER

CHAPTER 14: GOODBYE, SUZANNE SALINGER

One of the most important lessons I've learned is: Try very hard not to lose touch with good people in your life, people you care about, you enjoy, people whose lives have mattered to you. Even when your life gets very busy (or whatever), find a way to stay connected or make sure you reconnect before too much time goes by.

Sometimes there is no more time.

I learned this lesson most profoundly from my friendship with Suzanne Salinger. Of all people—the friend who brought me so much joy and fun, good conversations, her father Pierre, and the heavenly weekend at the Kennedy Compound. A friendship of multiple years—and then, somehow, we lost touch. Nothing bad happened between us. I think something very good happened to her. She'd been dating a man around the time of the Kennedy Compound visit, and I think they may have gotten more serious. But I draw a blank about the details.

I got so busy with my White House job, which started six months after Hyannis Port, that I wasn't much of a friend to any of my friends during those two years. But it also feels like Suzanne didn't even live near D.C. during my final years in the city. We didn't have any farewell meals or drinks while I was in the throes of permanently leaving D.C. for California in late

1982. I think she and her guy were busy with their life together wherever they lived.

All I know for sure is the following: In 2004, I heard on the news that Pierre Salinger had died at his home in France at the age of 79. I immediately thought *I must find Suzanne to express my sorrow and support. And say:* let's get our lives reconnected!

I would never have imagined what I learned next.

Pierre's obituary—in 2004—said his only daughter Suzanne had died of cancer in **1995**. She had been dead for nine years. My jaw dropped. My eyes filled with tears.

Suzanne and I were both born in 1951. I realized she'd just turned 44 when she died. I thought about how much life I'd experienced in the previous nine years and thus how much life she'd missed. I realized during all my dramatic times in 1994 and 1995 with vertigo and a buckling leg, Dr. Cathleen Schmitt, my first brain and spine MRI, and the verified MS diagnosis, Suzanne was fighting for her life.

According to news accounts I subsequently found, Suzanne was undergoing cancer treatment in 1995 and working for Air France at Dulles Airport in Virginia until she became too weak to work anymore.

CHAPTER 14: GOODBYE, SUZANNE SALINGER

She died at Georgetown University Hospital in Washington on October 25, 1995, the same hospital where Barbara Gamarekian would die in 2004—the same year Pierre Salinger died in France.

The news got even more stunning.

I'm not sure what year, but Suzanne had married at some point and, in 1984, given birth to twin sons named Justin and Joshua. The boys' surname (at least later on) was Salinger. Suzanne had seemingly gotten divorced somewhere along the way. I read more about Justin and Joshua and realized they were not quite eleven when she died. So, they were 10 and likely younger when she first got sick and started cancer treatment. How awful for everyone, I kept thinking. I couldn't find much information about the boys' father except that he had died five years after Pierre, in 2009. Suzanne must have been so worried about her young sons and their future as she struggled to get well and keep her job. I read that Pierre and his French wife had moved back to Washington and wondered if they'd returned to help Suzanne and their grandsons during this dreadful period. I wished I could have helped.

I could barely absorb all the traumas.

I then wondered what had happened to Pierre's mother, my wondrous Jehanne Bietry Salinger-Carlson. I read she had died five months *after* her granddaughter Suzanne, in March 1996. She was a few weeks shy of her 99th birthday. Her heart must have broken.

I recently learned Suzanne's cousin, the son of Pierre's brother Herbert, and his wife welcomed Suzanne's sons into their family after Suzanne's death. What a wonderful lifeline. Suzanne must have beamed relief and gratitude from Heaven.

I'm so pleased to say I understand her sons — now in their thirties — are doing well. Suzanne has grandchildren!

Part of the reason I decided to write this book was to honor Suzanne and to thank her for what she gave to my life. Her life here on earth mattered to many people. Her life mattered so much to me. What fun we had! And because of her, I was able to glide to my most shimmering dreams.

Rest in peace, my friend.

CHAPTER 15

HOW I REMEMBER MADELEINE ALBRIGHT

*This was my tribute
to Madeleine that I sent
to my family and friends
after her death in 2022*

CHAPTER 15: HOW I REMEMBER MADELEINE ALBRIGHT

Betty and I were driving around Marin County yesterday and I noticed flags were at half-staff on certain buildings. President Joe Biden made sure Madeleine Albright was so honored this week in 2022. What if a little bird had whispered in my ear in 1976 that one day, say, in 2022, the U.S. Senator for whom I was the first intern would be President of the United States and Madeleine Albright, my co-worker in Senator Edmund Muskie's office, whose desk was right near mine, a woman who shared personal vulnerabilities with me, would be honored the world over during her life and now, with her death. Say what, little birdie? *Get out of here!*

Such grandness was not only too much for anyone to imagine then, but also mitigated by my initial perceptions of Madeleine, which were not good. Madeleine Korbel Albright, fourteen years my senior, had an impressive background I would eventually learn (Ph.D. from Columbia, whose professor and mentor there, Dr. Zbigniew Brzezinski, as well as his daughter, Mika, would one day also hit the world's stage; a Czech-American diplomat for a father, Dr. Josef Korbel; and married to Joseph Medill Patterson Albright—descendant of a grand family of journalists and owners of New York newspapers, whose aunt married Harry Frank Guggenheim of, yes, *that* Guggenheim family. Whoa! But I would only bit-by-bit learn such things.

Defying Adversity as I Race to Achieve My Dreams

What struck me first was Madeleine's seeming innocence about office politics and toxic staff members. She'd been hired as Senator Muskie's chief Legislative Assistant and was kind of the head of my department. I never thought of her as my boss, though (I reported in my role as Legislative Correspondent to another Legislative Assistant). Whatever her responsibilities, I (and others) were floored by her quite vocally seeming to go along with the scheming plans to derail the job of our Office Manager, Leslie Finn, that were being instigated by a fellow Muskie staff member named Lorraine. I also really liked and admired Leslie, who had hired me. I decided the best thing to do was to tell Leslie. Leslie and many other staffers knew the otherwise brilliant, hard-working Lorraine could be verbally vicious. She frequently ridiculed and tried to derail people. Madeleine was doing her reputation no favors by seemingly playing into Lorraine's hands, as well as possibly hurting Leslie's career. (Leslie had just had a baby and was trying to establish her job as temporarily part-time.)

My talk with Leslie was made easy by Leslie's savvy and personal confidence. She assured me Madeleine would never know my role and that I'd done the right thing. A few days later, Leslie called me into her office and said the problem had been solved. She and the Chief of Staff had had a talk with Madeleine.

CHAPTER 15: HOW I REMEMBER MADELEINE ALBRIGHT

Problem fixed. And, amazingly, all the talking and scheming stopped. 100%. Poof. I've never seen anything like it. I've read several of Madeleine's books and I think her new Muskie job, at age nearly 38, might have been her first. She got a Ph.D. and started raising her three daughters and may have been entering the workforce a decade or more after most other employed women. For all her intellectual smarts, I think she might have had to play catch-up with the real office world. Someone like Lorraine would smell naïve blood.

I also now realize Madeleine's seemingly serene, calm demeanor, along with her always-direct eyes looking at you (she is exactly the same in person as on TV) can give an impression of agreement with what you're saying but may simply be her look while gathering information.

I think Madeleine readily *got it* when Leslie and the Chief of Staff laid it all out to her. I bet they talked to Lorraine, too, and put her job on the line. I don't think Lorraine could have gone so silent so quickly otherwise. I used to be embarrassed about setting this up—sending Madeleine Albright "to the woodshed"—and nervous Madeleine would find out. But I now feel pretty good about it. I smile a little sheepishly when I watch footage of Madeleine with world leaders dealing with critically important world issues. But office politics count, too.

Brings sentimental tears now, looking at flags of a nation saying thank you and goodbye to her.

I would come quite quickly thereafter to appreciate Madeleine's intelligence and other admirable traits. I still see her more than anything as a hugely talented person with deep vulnerabilities. She is quite open in her books about some of these vulnerabilities, so I don't think she'd mind if I tell you about a couple. I think she wanted people and especially young girls and women to know a woman who has coped with harsh personal issues can still be a great success in the world in all sorts of endeavors and live a very happy and fulfilled life. Here we go:

Weight Watchers was all the rage in the 1970s and several branches were opening throughout D.C. Madeleine, as ever, was wanting to lose weight and decided she'd try a Weight Watchers near her (fabulous) home in the posh Georgetown section of Washington. Forty pounds off was her goal. I decided to try the Capitol Hill Weight Watchers near my apartment. Twenty pounds. Anyone else? A middle-aged staffer named Mark threw his hat in the ring, too. Mark was the first to tell you he weighed around 400 pounds. He looked like former New Jersey

CHAPTER 15: HOW I REMEMBER MADELEINE ALBRIGHT

governor Chris Christie at his heaviest. He was going for 200 pounds at whatever Weight Watchers was near his home. Madeleine (40), Jenny (20), and Mark (200) all started the same day. A few weeks in, Madeleine rushed over to my desk with a stricken look. "What?!" I asked. "Mark just told me it's really good I'm on Weight Watchers. I'm not as heavy as he is, am I?"

I was so moved and kind of intrigued (little did I know I would end my working life as a counselor at Jenny Craig for 18 years). Mark casually threw out his weight goal, 400 to 200, as if it were in the category of "I need to lose 40" and then said such a thing to Madeleine. She seemed to really believe at some level she was the person weighing 400 pounds. I tried to reassure her. (And kudos to Mark, who did lose 200 pounds.)

Several years later, I was invited to a party at the home of Bob Torricelli, who worked with me on Vice President Walter Mondale's staff and was running for a congressional seat from New Jersey (which he won). I looked over and there was Madeleine. She'd never been so svelte. I smiled and started to approach her. She gave me a **Don't** look. I knew something bad must have happened. I wondered if cancer had produced the weight loss. I would shortly hear that her husband Joe, father of her three daughters, had ended their marriage, saying he'd fallen in love with someone else and then had added complaints about Madeleine's looks. **Daggers to the heart**.

About a decade later, Madeleine would become Ambassador to the United Nations and then Secretary of State — the highest rank at the time of any woman in U.S. history. **Pick yourself up**. **Then You Go, Girl!**

I think, too, about Madeleine's giddy glow as she returned to Muskie's office after spending some unexpected moments with actor Robert Redford in his glory days. He'd come to D.C. to give Senator Muskie some environmental award. Madeleine had to discreetly bend down to whisper something in (the seated) Robert Redford's ear. She said she nearly fainted as his handsome face looked at her!

I remember when we Muskie staffers thought it was such a big deal that Madeleine sometimes went out to lunch with the founding head of the new Congressional Budget Office, Alice Rivlin. So impressive! (*You're way higher now, Madeleine!*)

I remember FBI agents coming to Senator Muskie's office when President Carter appointed Madeleine head of Congressional Relations and the FBI had to clear her for the role. Ha! We confidently said all

CHAPTER 15: HOW I REMEMBER MADELEINE ALBRIGHT

good things to them. Wow, Madeleine. The White House. *(Can we visit you?!)*

I remember asking if you'd serve as a reference for me as I pitched a job on that same White House staff a year later—for Vice President Mondale's Advance Coordinator. You said you'd be delighted. Damn, I can't find the list of my references—but there you would be, your name, your home address, your home phone number, your White House phone number. *You hadn't yet required confidentiality.*

You knocked it out of the ballpark, Madeleine Korbel Albright. Your daughters, their husbands, and your grandchildren adore you, too. Friends galore.

Off you go now to somewhere over the rainbow where blue birds fly.

CHAPTER 16

APPRECIATING CLINT HILL

Former Secret Service Agent Clint Hill and his co-author wife Lisa McCubbin Hill addressed a large audience at Book Passage, located near their home in Northern California, on November 18, 2023. The focus of the event was the recent update of Mr. Hill's 2013 memoir, "Five Days in November," with its account of the days before, during, and after the assassination of President John F. Kennedy on November 22, 1963. The event also served as an acknowledgment of the upcoming sixtieth anniversary of that tragic day in Dallas.

Secret Service Agent Clint Hill was riding in the presidential motorcade that day, in a car immediately behind President and Mrs. Kennedy's limousine. He witnessed the impact of the shots and ran to the limousine to protect President and Mrs. Kennedy by putting his body over them. He later received an official citation for "exceptional bravery" for his actions that day.

The author of this memoir is deeply moved to have met Clint Hill and Lisa McCubbin Hill while attending Book Passage events honoring their books about his career as a Secret Service agent for five U.S. presidents. Mr. Hill's wife was instrumental in encouraging him to write about his career and his special professional relationship with both President John F. Kennedy and First Lady Jacqueline Kennedy.

Jennifer ("Jenny") Wood, the author of this book, a memoir that highlights her own connection to the Kennedy family and the impact of November 22,

1963, on her life, appreciates the "symmetry" of her meeting Clint Hill and reading his books as that milestone anniversary approached and as her own book was being published. In a life where the Kennedys or Kennedy-affiliated people have unexpectedly popped into her life, the author enjoys knowing the Secret Service agent who was raised in North Dakota and spent many years in Washington, D.C. later in life married Lisa McCubbin, a woman who had settled in Northern California. The couple then moved into a house very close to the author's. All three frequent the same acclaimed local bookstore, a bookstore that has proudly carried all of their books over the years.

EPILOGUE

EPILOGUE

It's amazing how things sometimes appear just when we need them. A woman's philosophy of life was recently included in her obituary in my local newspaper. She believed:

> **"No matter what life deals you,**
> **accept it with positive grace,**
> **challenge it,**
> **and**
> **for God's sake, follow your dreams!"**

I like this! What do you think?

I initially paused over the "accept with positive grace" line. I'm not a fan of rushes to forgive the unrepentant and believe anger at the likes of rapists and dismissive doctors is justified — and necessary — if we ever want to inspire improvements.

But I gather this is where the "challenge it" comes in.

I don't feel anger about getting MS. I feel it about how I was treated by all those initial doctors. So, I guess I feel "positive grace" at finally being correctly diagnosed and about my MS infusions. I am now "challenging" the medical profession to help doctors improve their diagnostic process and other communications with their patients.

Remember "Uncle Walter" from the beginning of this book? He was a physician and our family friend who had terminal cancer. When my mother visited him in the hospital, he sighed, "Oh, Ann, what I have learned, what I have learned." I wonder if what he had learned is what I'm now hoping to convey.

I think a light went off in Uncle Walter's head while he was a seriously ill patient in the hospital, an enlightenment illustrating how doctors can sometimes be so smart and then so deficient in understanding what patients really need at a given time. Some doctors can be so helpful and then so (seemingly, unwittingly) harmful. They appear to grasp their *full* responsibilities to patients, but then devolve into behaviors or communications that just don't cut it.

This is different from being a busy physician rushing between patients. It is more fundamental: it's about how a doctor usually *interacts* with his or her patients; how doctors *feel* about their patients; how doctors *convey* their *feelings*.

Do some doctors feel they need to *play a role* with their patients, perhaps to come across as more **authoritative**? It can appear that way sometimes. That puts the emphasis on the doctor, often at the expense of what's best for the patient. For example,

EPILOGUE

some doctors can come across as **Very confident, Very busy** *scientists*, when *the patient really needs* a knowledgeable, yet obviously *caring guide*; or as the patient's **taskmaster**, rather than an engaged listener and questioner trying to provide the best help; or as a **suspicious cop**, rather than a doctor who is thoughtful without being condescending.

More thoughtful and respectful exchanges tend to inspire more trusting and honest communications between patients and their doctors. This promotes better healing.

I bet Uncle Walter, being a doctor-patient among doctors, and so very ill, suddenly recognized the *health* **benefits** of **doctors** (and *not* **just nurses**) actually *nurturing* their patients at least a little bit more. **Slow down just a bit**, Docs, maybe spend a little quiet time with a hospitalized patient, a hand on a patient's shoulder, a **warm expression** in your eyes. No need to always talk. No need to always be the authority figure, the person in charge. Instead, *quietly convey a gentle understanding of what the patient is experiencing.* It can mean so much.

Emotional Intelligence is very real and crucial when interacting with patients. Having and displaying empathy, "good bedside manners," actually **listening**, and **showing** genuine *caring and respect* **for patients** can be as important to the healing process as prescribing medications and performing surgeries.

Most nurses seem to know this. Studies show the empathy of nurses is hugely important to the healing process. **Doctors need to include these behaviors** in their "medicine bags" as well — and *use them*.

I sometimes wonder what my early doctors (now all deceased) would say if they learned their former patient Jenny Wood did indeed have MS all those years ago. I'd love to see the expressions on their faces if they could see my MRI results. My burning, tingling, crawling skin was actually happening because of very real nerve destruction. Ditto my double vision, blind spot, fading colors and other eye disturbances. Doctor after doctor told me nothing was medically wrong, not MS, not any other medical disease. Not a single doctor suggested I get **another opinion**, either within the original physician's field or from other specialists (*except mental health*, in an era when it could be job-threatening for patients to receive mental health treatment). Nor did any doctor **offer** to make any **referrals**. Why? This can expand knowledge and offer relief from possibly strained doctor-patient relations.

The message from most of my doctors came across as: you mustn't waste a doctor's time. You don't have a real disease. We know, you don't. Take care. Goodbye.

I had to learn how to survive *my doctors*. It is so frightening and discouraging to learn from all the nurses I talked to during my 2021 hospitalization, plus from many books, that significant problems still exist, especially between male physicians and their female patients. **Maybe we need more** *malpractice* **suits to inspire better doctoring**. If more effective MS medications had existed back then, my doctors' dismissiveness could constitute malpractice. I kiss the ground MRI scanners stand on. MRI results provide patients with validation, a stronger voice. They can serve as beacons for a patient's knowledge and bravery. We knew. *And we were right.*

"AND FOR GOD'S SAKE, FOLLOW YOUR DREAMS!"

I just love this advice from the aforementioned obituary. In writing this book, I more clearly than ever realize how this philosophy actually propelled my life.

The themes of the Kennedy family involving courage and approaching life as an adventure resonated with me from the get-go. It made life exciting and gave me the drive and energy to pursue goals. More than I could have imagined, it kept me from despair when my life's expected trajectory went terribly awry on several occasions. Instead, it inspired moxie, grit, tenacity, and resilience.

Finding our dreams, our passions, is so important, whatever they may be. Go after them! This process then tends to take on a life of its own.

I was a professionally ambitious female growing up in the 1950s and 1960s. I embraced the growing trend of no marriage or children until later in life.

I joined the trend of young women insisting they be able to travel to the likes of Europe without male accompaniment.

I wanted, and achieved, a career as a Washington, D.C. staffer for important leaders and lived alone in my own exciting apartment on Capitol Hill. I created my dream life.

I believed the world would eventually accept that women could do all of this. There is terrible sexism and misogyny, but *just watch us go!*

EPILOGUE

Everything went perfectly—beyond my dreams—during the first nine months of 1973. I was so happy. So proud of myself.

Then nightmares began: Horror in France, awful physical problems, dismissive doctors, mental health doubts, homophobia fears. Was I going psycho? Was my life falling apart? Is this some kind of test? Can't women handle it? Oh, God, maybe it's me! It certainly felt like a train wreck. From heaven to hell in just a few months. Almost everywhere I turned over the next decade or two, it felt as if I hit a brick wall or fell into a hole. As my father said, I became a rat caught in a maze.

But, in the end, I won. I'm stronger and wiser than I knew. I believed in myself and had family support. I, not the initial doctors, diagnosed my disease correctly. They failed at everything: wrong assessment, poor communication, and a pathetic diagnostic process. There is no excuse. I hope my suggestions about how to improve the diagnostic process are helpful. *The medical profession still needs it badly.*

I hope the philanthropists Melinda French Gates, MacKenzie Scott, and others will earmark significant sums for the study of **autoimmune disease,** a category that has included Multiple Sclerosis for many years. The various autoimmune diseases mostly affect females. Such diseases have long presented diagnostic and treatment challenges. You can bet the female element plays a role. **Multiple books show the prejudice against believing women still lives.** Maybe this is sexism rearing its ugly head. Or maybe it's due at least in part to forgetting or minimizing the fact that males and females have very different bodies.

Almost unbelievably, health and physiology research continues to be performed mostly on males — that is, mostly on White Males. I just finished reading one of the most important books of my life (both male and female Amazon book reviewers agree). The book is entitled, *Invisible Women: Data Bias in a World Designed for Men,* by Caroline Criado Perez. This is *not* some irate feminist screed. Nor is its focus solely on healthcare issues. It involves deep and wide scholarly research on the data collection process of pretty much everything we decide to study in our increasingly data-driven world. The book's data could be overwhelming if it weren't presented in the author's skillful, interesting, and witty way. The only "overwhelm" is recognizing how dangerous (downright stupid and uncaring) our data collection process continues to be.

EPILOGUE

Male bodies, male hormones, average male height and weight, average male fat and muscle distribution, male body parts, etc. are considered the norm—the default mode—for data collection and analysis purposes. **Females (half the population of the world)** are considered "other/atypical" or simply "smaller men" for most research purposes. Studies of female bodies, their average height and weight, female hormones, female body parts, etc. play a small role in these studies—if they are considered at all. Policy/production decisions are then made—based on the **male results**—pronouncements about how a disease typically presents, what medicines work—or don't work—and at what dosages. Serious design flaws can occur where other research subjects are concerned. Relying only on male results to, let's say, determine appliance sizes and shapes, has led to appliances that fit the typically larger and stronger male hand, while failing to meet many female requirements. God forbid what Artificial Intelligence will cause if these deficits and miscalculations continue.

One can more clearly see how medical schools and medical books can teach incomplete or totally inaccurate information to doctors, especially about female health issues.

Males and females differ from one another in significant ways. Machismo tends to relish this fact. I think *a whole lot* of machismo caused *the whole lot* of my initial doctors to make their blatantly erroneous assumptions and pronouncements.

We've got to stop this. Substantial research on females must be required. Then male versus female test results must be separated, documented, and correctly applied. Only then should we make decisions about the efficacy of medications (and the like) for each gender, with recommended dosages. Many male and female reviewers strongly encourage people to read *Invisible Women: Data Bias in a World Designed for Men*. It provides an education about what is wrong and why. And its lessons can help us **all**.

Wow! I've got to add this. I woke up this morning (early 2024) and felt jubilant. I'd had a dream the previous night that I'd met a woman who possessed great knowledge and wisdom (and a wonderful sense of humor). She and I had had similar medical experiences that brought forth almost eerily similar reactions in both of us. Her insights about the medical profession's weaknesses so closely matched mine, I felt renewed confidence in my conclusions about what Uncle Walter was trying to tell my mother when he, a physician dying from cancer, lamented, "Oh, what I have learned, what I have learned."

EPILOGUE

Then it struck me, that wasn't a dream! That was the book I had just read: *All In Her Head. The Truth and Lies Early Medicine Taught Us About Women's Bodies and Why It Matters Today,* by Elizabeth Comen, MD. More than ever, the psychological defense mechanism of "projection" cried out: how a person or group of people attribute characteristics they fear or hate in themselves to other individuals or groups.

What an important book, Dr. Comen. I think our books ought to dance with each other.

In yet another example of important things that can show up at just the right time, I discovered *The New York Times* published the following from columnist Zeynep Tufekci on August 28, 2022:

> "Medicine doesn't like what it can't understand, so it often ignores it," Ravindra Ganesh, a physician scientist who directs post-Covid care at the Mayo Clinic, told me. It's increasingly clear that post-viral conditions are key to understanding many illnesses.
>
> "People with multiple sclerosis were once told they had a conversion disorder — the historic catchall for 'It's in your head, dear.' Later, advances in imaging allowed cerebral lesions to be seen. Genetic and environmental

conditions were later invoked as possible causes. However, this year a multi-decade study showed something that was previously met with skepticism: Multiple sclerosis follows from infections by the Epstein-Barr virus, sometimes decades later[....]

"Then there's myalgic encephalomyelitis/chronic fatigue syndrome, an ailment that can leave previously healthy people bedbound and severely limit their physical or cognitive abilities. As many as three-quarters of [these] patients trace their illness to an infection. But these patients have long been battling neglect and suspicion, with minuscule research devoted to the condition[....]

"The science of post-viral conditions is complex and little understood. It involves the immune system, autoimmune conditions, neuropsychiatry, cardiovascular and metabolic systems and viruses themselves[....] We need a National Institute for Post-viral Conditions, similar to the National Cancer Institute, to oversee and integrate research [....] Such an agency would let us finally tell the sufferers that help is on the way."

EPILOGUE

I personally don't recall ever having an Epstein-Barr infection. It's certainly possible. I bet MS comes from a variety of processes, perhaps a "perfect storm" of things. I am greatly relieved that medical science is at least moving in the right direction—meaning in the *opposite* direction of where I began.

I'm grateful for the many fine physicians who are now part of my life or who, such as Dr. Cathleen Schmitt and Dr. James Kelly, combined their diagnosis of my case of Multiple Sclerosis in 1995 with their superior medical attention and caring. My now worsening case of MS contains the silver lining of excellent guidance and treatment recommendations from Dr. Lynda Lam, Kaiser Permanente Neurologist, and Dr. Wilbur Leong, Kaiser MS Pharmacist. Who could have guessed receiving Rituximab immunosuppressive infusions at Kaiser's Infusion Center in San Rafael, California every six months would become even a pleasant experience for me? Really! There's nothing like a professional team providing beneficial treatments while pampering you. "Would you like another warm blanket?" one nurse asked me recently. "Thanks. I'd love one," I responded. Then I added, "How about a martini, too?" "Oh, wouldn't that be nice!" she laughed.

After a half-century, I knew my health issues—my Multiple Sclerosis issues—were at last being treated seriously, and with deep caring, by the medical profession. A ray of sunshine suddenly burst through one of the many windows of the appealing Infusion Center. I sat back and thought, This is good. It's really good. I've been waiting for this kind of treatment for a long, long time.

ACKNOWLEDGMENTS

I doubt I would have ever written a memoir if my friend Gerri Alaniz hadn't so kindly encouraged me. Once I got going, I realized it was just what I needed to do. I also want to thank my relatives and friends who said I should write another book and the nurses during my 2021 hospitalization who urged me to publicize my medical experiences from the 1970s onward. You gave me the courage to proceed.

Writing this book has given me an opportunity to honor special people in my work life. My profound thanks to Vice President Walter Mondale's Deputy Chief of Staff, Michael S. Berman, for his strong support of me. May you rest in peace, Mike. I want to further acknowledge several people associated with the Mondale Advance Office who were especially meaningful to me: my beloved Arnot Edwin Walker, Kate Sheaffer, and Chuck Campion. They each went on to even greater career and life achievements and all of them left this world way too soon. And here's to the late great author (and my fellow realtor friend), Kevin Cash: *Here's Looking at **You**, Kevin.*

Joanne Stover, thank you for your contributions to this book and to my life. You were a double bonus when I met your mother, Dolores. Then there's Kristin Hite, whose deep reach into my family's history has brought us many smiles. Newly discovered cousin Angie Ferris, too. Thank you both! To Eileen, Kathy, and Cyndi…we met as toddlers and I'm so glad we're still deeply meaningful to one another. And here's to Micheline and Lizette and other friends I met long after toddlerhood but who remain such a special part of my life. I'm so grateful for *all* my friends.

Cynthia L. Stanley, MFT, I want to say, *Thank you for everything*. Do you agree I found a heavenly spot for your Sigmund Freud comment?

To the late Dr. Walter W. Dolfini: I so hope I captured your deeply-felt concerns.

Huge thanks to my sister, Elizabeth Boutelle Wood Lawrence (aka "Liz"), and my partner, Betty Hirschfeld, for lovingly reading my book manuscript and offering important insights. I also feel fortunate to once again receive the expertise of Ruth Schwartz, founder and CEO of Wonderlady Books. From your guidance around the title, creating the marvelous front cover, the thoughtful editing by you and Curt Kinkead, *Defying Adversity as I Race to Achieve My Dreams* and I say, *Thank You*, Ruth.

To President Joseph Biden, Senator Edmund Muskie, and Vice President Walter Mondale: **My 12-year-old self (and my older one) will forever glow in gratitude to you.**

I dedicated my *Uncle Harold* book to my partner, Betty Hirschfeld, and my parents, Ann and Frank Wood. This memoir highlights my devotion to my siblings, Cathy, Mitch, Kent, and Liz, and their partners, Don, Deborah, and Darryl, and my magical friend, Suzanne Salinger. But since Mom and Dad and Betty are essential to what has comprised love and joy and gratitude in my life, this is of course for them as well.

www.ingramcontent.com/pod-product-compliance
Lightning Source LLC
Chambersburg PA
CBHW070534010526
44118CB00012B/1137